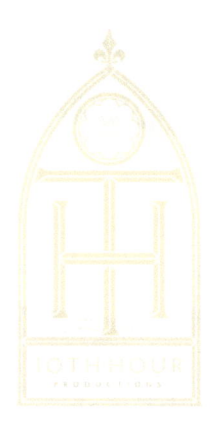

Copyright © 2024 10th Hour Productions

All rights reserved. No part of this book may be reproduced or used in any manner without written permission of the copyright owner except for the use of quotations in a book review.

Excerpt from *The Return of the Prodigal Son* printed with permission by Penguin Random House LLC

ISBN 979-8-3507-2685-5

A publication of 10th Hour Productions
www.wildgoose.tv
www.10thhourproductions.org

Author
Fr. Dave Pivonka TOR

Editor
Philip Martin

Layout and Design
Courtney Silvernail and Mary Patterson Wallace

Photography
Nick Staresinic and Dan Johnson

CONTENTS

A Good Father	1
Earthly Fathers	23
Sons & Daughters	45
A Holy Family	67
Priestly Fatherhood	89
The Father Waits	111
Resources	133

A Good Father

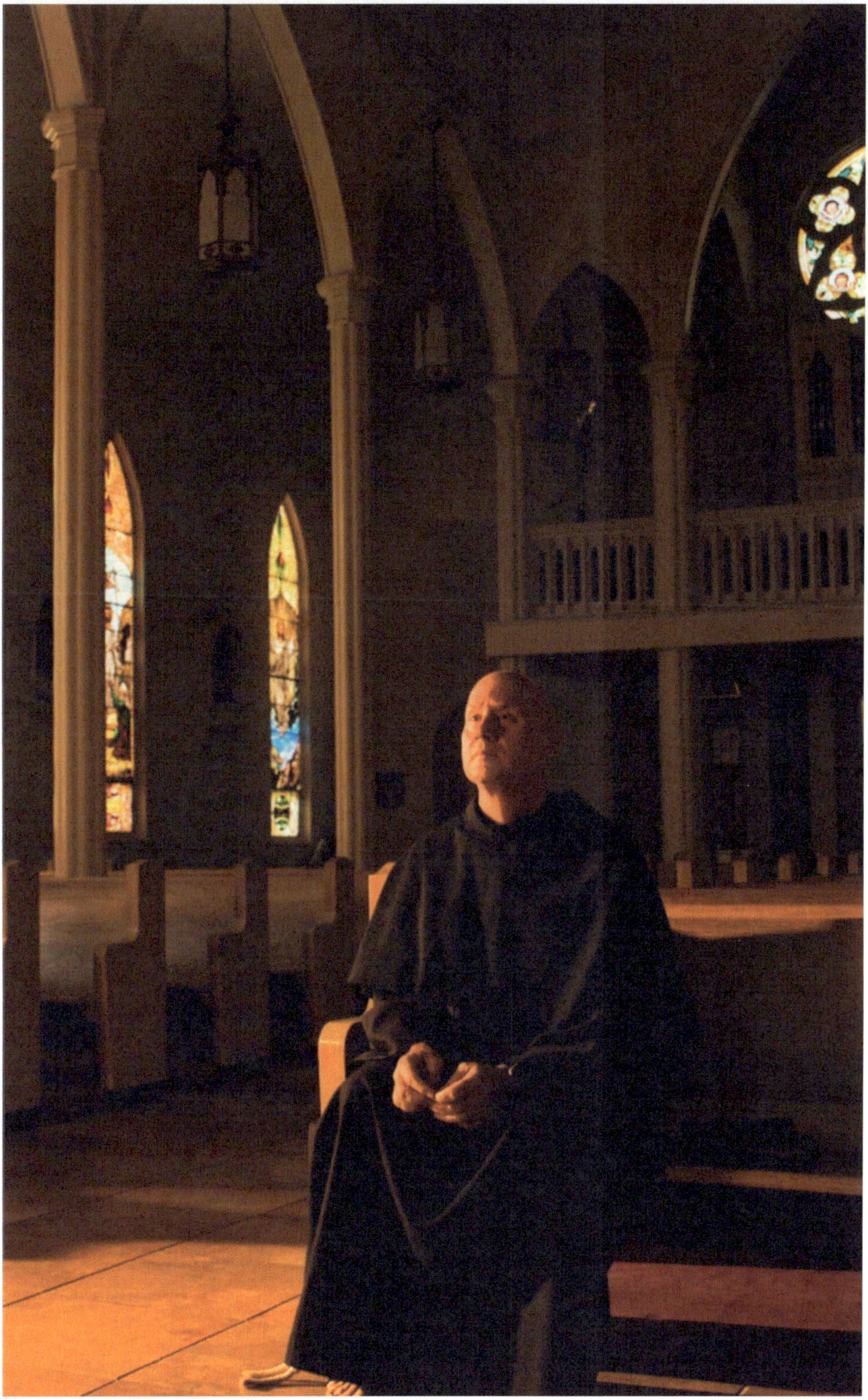

A GOOD FATHER
EPISODE 1

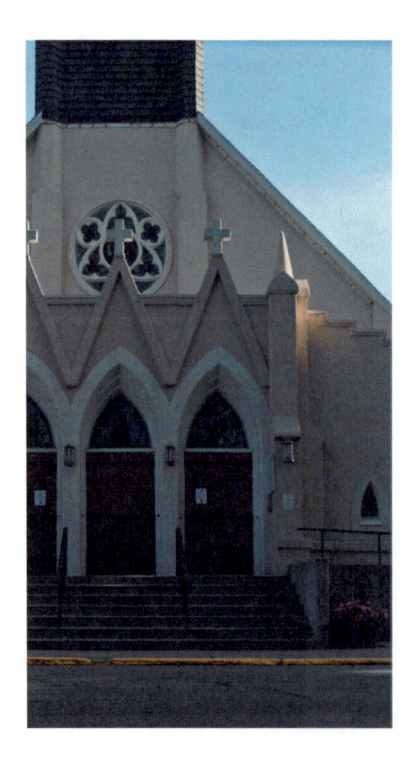

SYNOPSIS

God is Father, and Jesus came to reveal God as Father. Even in a worldly crisis of fatherhood, we are not orphans, we are not alone. God sees us, knows us, and loves us for who we are, not for what we can do. This life, however is a pilgrimage; we are journeying by grace to the house of the Father. Jesus, the Image of the Father, accompanies us on this journey, showing us the way by his grace and example. We are sons and daughters of a good Father.

"Have I been with you for so long a time and you still do not know me, Philip? Whoever has seen me has seen the Father."

- John 14:9 -

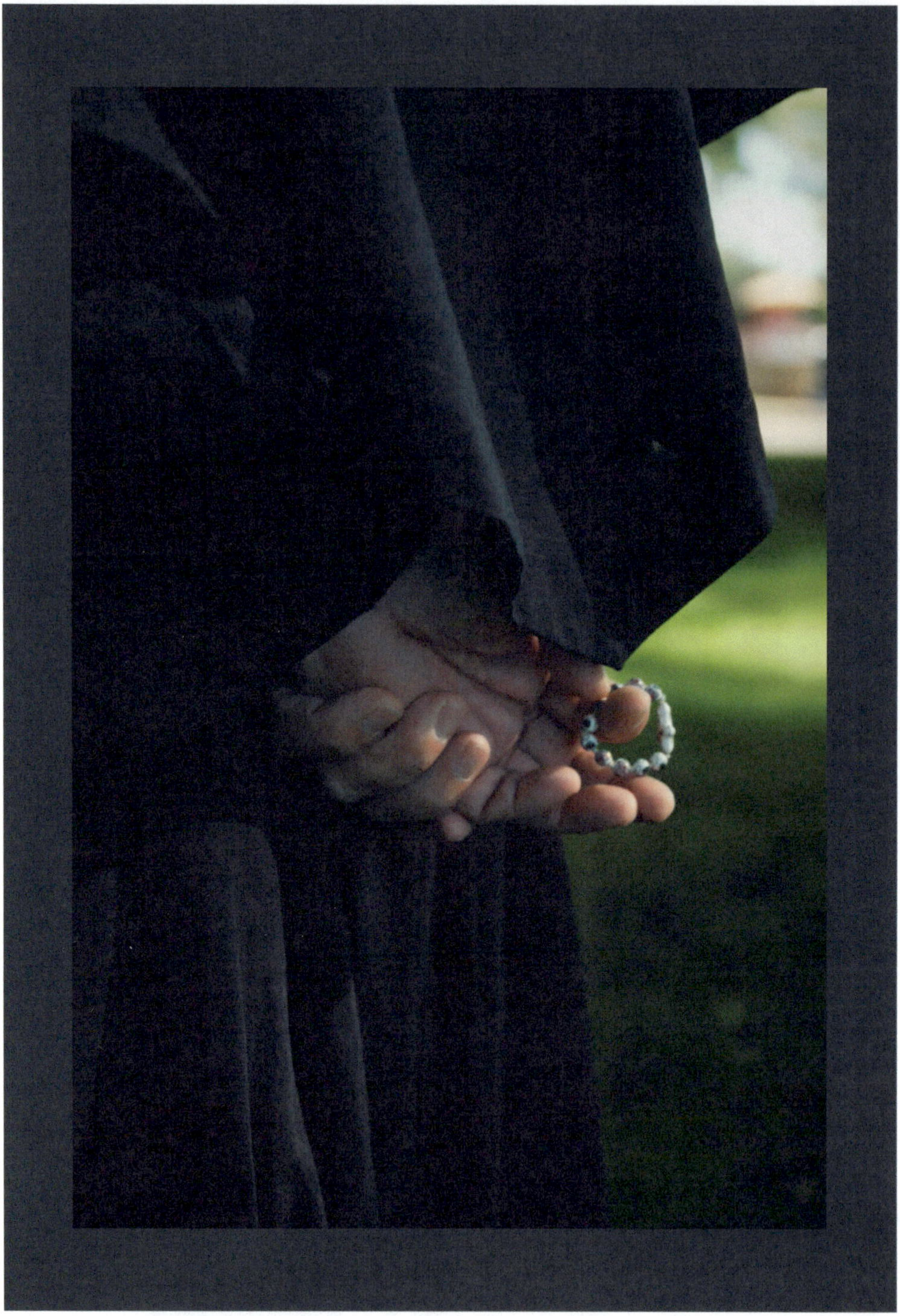

KEY TEXTS

"Look at the birds in the sky; they do not sow or reap, they gather nothing into barns, yet your heavenly Father feeds them. Are not you more important than they?" Matthew 6:26

SAINTS

St. Columba: "Alone with none but thee, my God, I journey on my way. What need I fear when thou art near, oh, king of night and day? More safe am I within thy hand, than if a host did round me stand."

St. John Paul II: "We are not the sum of our weaknesses and failures; we are the sum of the Father's love for us and our real capacity to become the image of his Son."

SCRIPTURE

Exodus 14:14: "The Lord himself will fight for you; you have only to keep still."

Matthew 6:6-7, 8b: "But when you pray, go to your inner room, close the door, and pray to your Father in secret. And your Father who sees in secret will repay you…Your Father knows what you need before you ask him."

John 17:25-26: "Righteous Father, the world also does not know you, but I know you, and they know that you sent me. I made known to them your name and I will make it known, that the love with which you loved me may be in them and I in them."

OTHER

Pope Francis: "Jesus Christ is the face of the Father's mercy."

CCC 239: "By calling God 'Father,' the language of faith indicates two main things: that God is the first origin of everything and transcendent authority; and that he is at the same time goodness and loving care for all his children."

"The whole of the Christian life is like a great pilgrimage to the house of the Father, whose unconditional love for every human creature, and in particular for the 'prodigal son', we discover anew each day. This pilgrimage takes place in the heart of each person…"

Pope Saint John Paul II

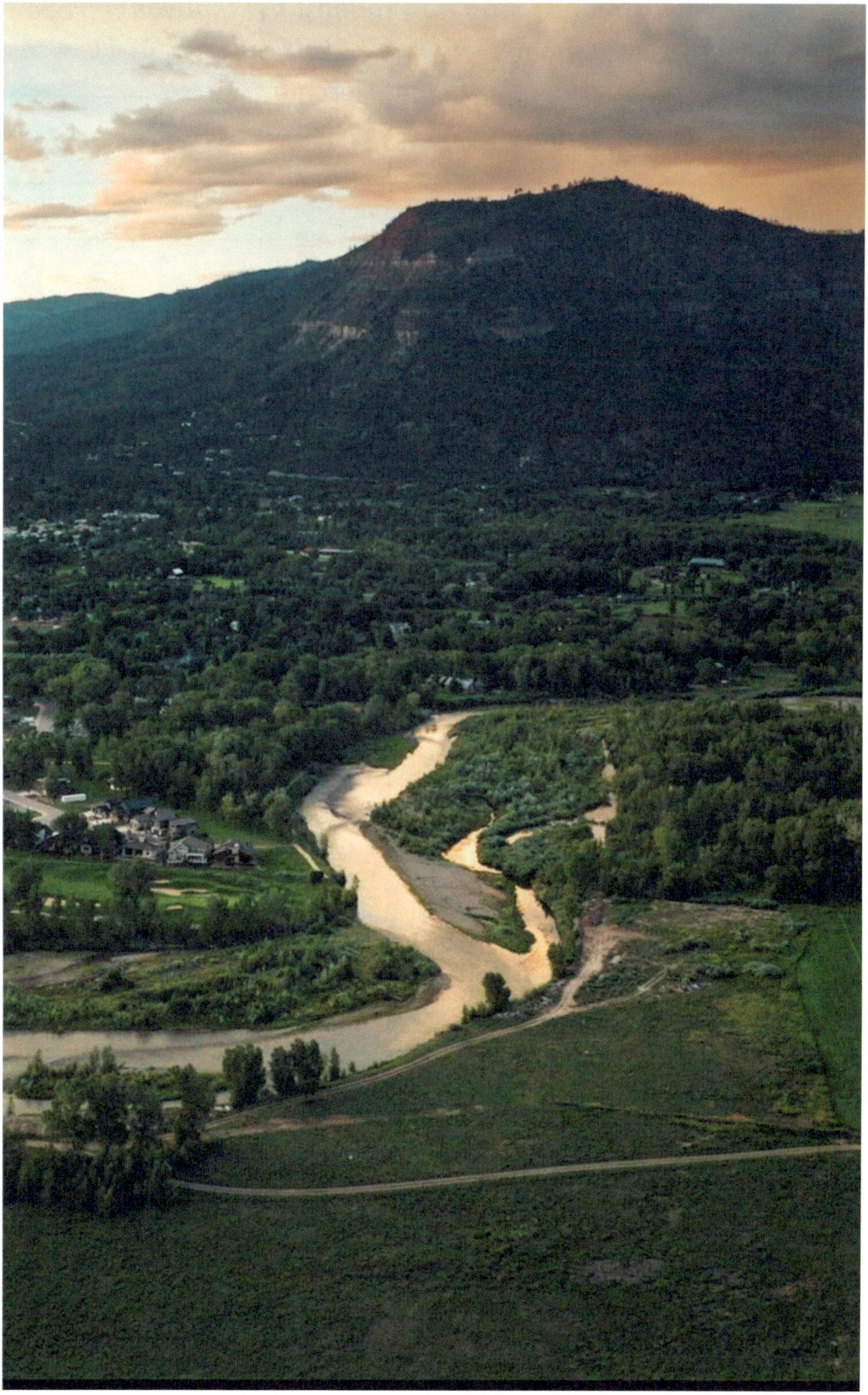

1. Under what circumstances do you most feel that you have to earn God's love, even though you know He freely gives it? How can you invite God into those circumstances?

_____
_____
_____
_____
_____
_____
_____
_____
_____
_____
_____
_____
_____
_____
_____
_____
_____

2. In a world that increasingly does not know the Love of the Father, how can you be an instrument of God's Love? Who, specifically, is the Holy Spirit calling you to minister to in this way? Ask Him to show you the means to do so.

_____
_____
_____
_____
_____
_____
_____
_____
_____
_____
_____
_____
_____
_____
_____
_____
_____

3. How can you invite Jesus into those moments in your life when you did not feel loved, or when you did not receive the love you deserve? How can Jesus show you this love today? Reflect on this in prayer.

_____

_____

_____

_____

_____

_____

_____

_____

_____

_____

_____

_____

_____

_____

_____

_____

"God our Father, make us really alive by giving us the light to know You, the only true God, and Jesus Christ Whom You have sent. Grant us the Holy Spirit and enable us to speak volumes about Your ineffable mysteries."

Pause for Prayer

PRAYER BY SERAPION OF THMUIS

GOING

Fr. Jacques Philippe says that God wants "happy sons and daughters" and He is eager to set us free. Why, then, does God allow us to be hurt and experience wounds? Can you think of a time when God filled in the cracks of your heart with His Living Water, more deeply revealing his Love as a Father?

_____
_____
_____
_____
_____
_____
_____
_____
_____
_____
_____
_____

DEEPER

In John 5:6, Jesus asks a sick man, "Do you want to be well?" In Episode 1, John Edwards speaks of having experienced healing by inviting Jesus into his memory, into his wound. What memory, what event, or what circumstance do you need to prayerfully give Jesus permission to enter into and heal?

_____
_____
_____
_____
_____
_____
_____
_____
_____
_____
_____
_____
_____

Katie Hartfiel speaks about her desire to be known and loved for who she is, but Dr. Breuninger spoke on the Central Relational Paradox: that we all have this desire, but we are afraid that, once seen and known, we will be abandoned. How does this truth affect your relationship with your loved ones (especially, if married, your spouse) and God? Why do our hearts think that entering into the Gaze of the Father will be painful, when our minds know that it is there that we will find peace and freedom?

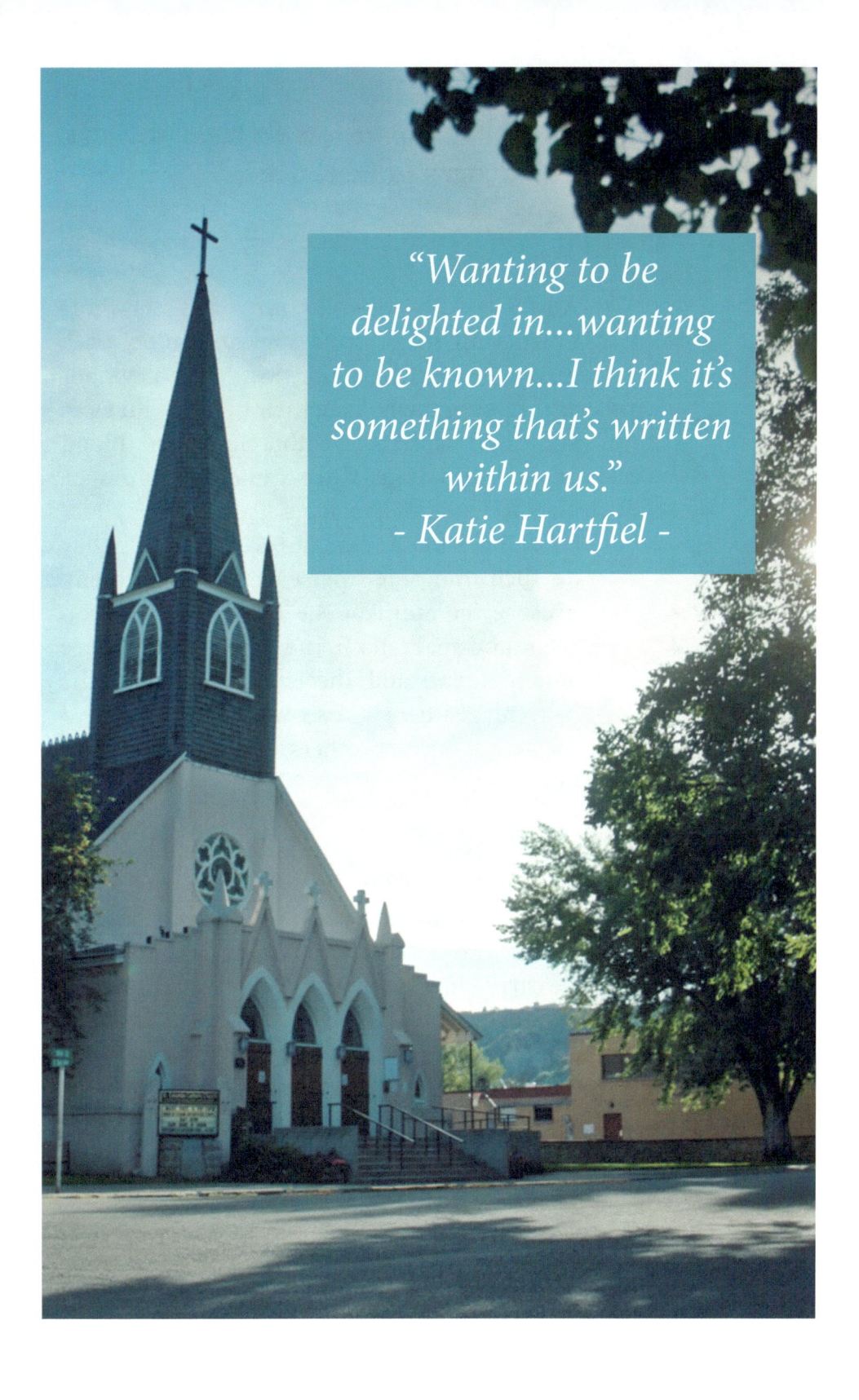

"Wanting to be delighted in...wanting to be known...I think it's something that's written within us."
- Katie Hartfiel -

Earlier Exhortation To the Brothers and Sisters of Penance

All those who love the Lord with their whole heart, with their whole soul and mind, with their whole strength and love their neighbor as themselves, who hate their bodies with vices and sins, who receive the Body and Blood of our Lord Jesus Christ, and who produce worthy fruits of penance. O how happy and blessed are these men and women while they do such things and persevere in doing them, because the Spirit of the Lord will rest upon them and make Its home and dwelling place among them, and they are children of the heavenly Father Whose works they do, and they are spouses, brothers, and mothers of our Lord Jesus Christ.

We are spouses when the faithful soul is joined by the Holy Spirit to our Lord Jesus Christ. We are brothers to Him when we do the will of the Father who is in heaven. We are mothers when we carry Him in our heart and body through a divine love and a pure and sincere conscience and give birth to Him through a holy activity which must shine as an example before others.

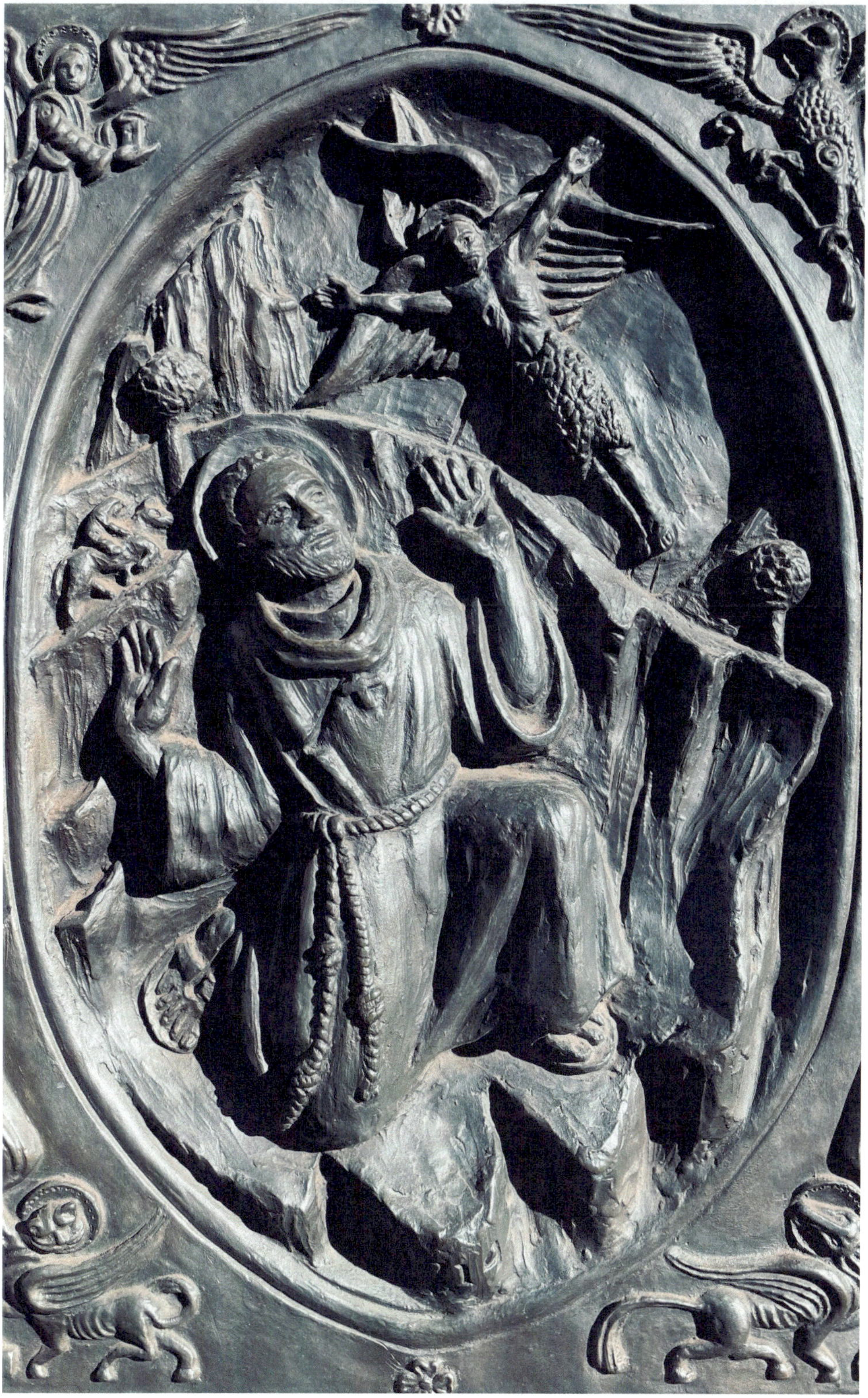

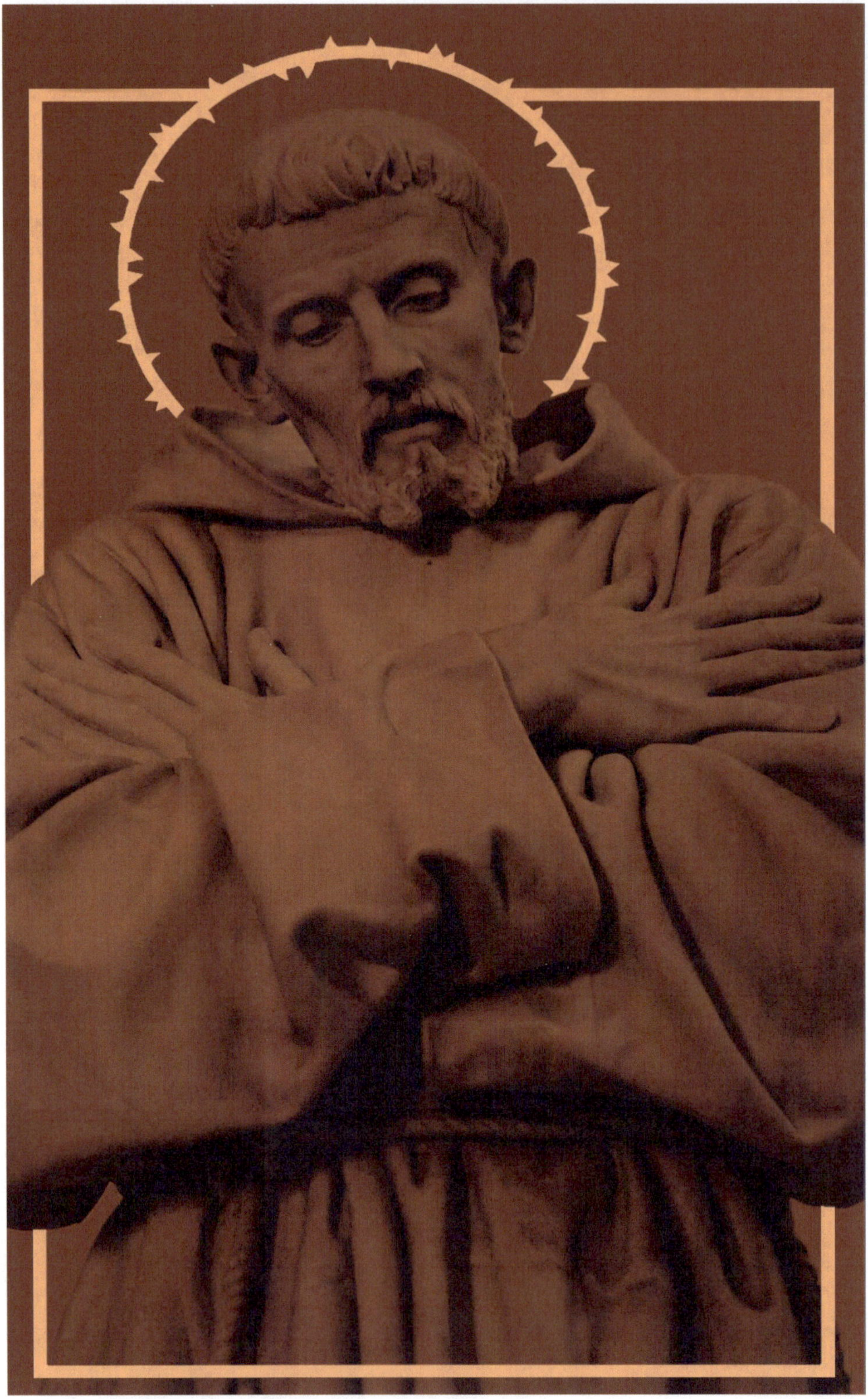

REFLECTION BY SAINT FRANCIS OF ASSISI

O how glorious it is to have a holy and great Father in heaven! O how holy, consoling to have such a beautiful and wonderful Spouse! O how holy and how loving, gratifying, humbling, peace-giving, sweet, worthy of love, and, above all things, desirable: to have such a Brother and such a Son, our Lord Jesus Christ, Who laid down his life for His sheep and prayed to His Father, saying:

Holy Father, in your name, save those whom you have given me in the world; they were yours and you gave them to me. The words that you gave to me I have given to them, and they accepted them and have believed in truth that I have come from you and they have known that you have sent me.

I pray for them and not for the world. Bless and sanctify them; I sanctify myself for them. I pray not only for them, but for those who will believe in me through their word that they might be sanctified in being one as we are.

I wish, Father, that where I am, they also may be with me that they may see my glory in your kingdom. Amen.

REFLECT

Come, Holy Spirit. Take some time when you are not distracted and in silence and thank God for being a Good Father. Invite Him to fill in the gaps that exist between what you have needed throughout your life (such as fatherly or motherly love, words and phrases of consolation and compliment, the right love in the right moments) and what you have received. He is close; He is a Good Father; He is not far off.

SENDING FORTH

We know by faith that God uses all that we have, all that we are, and all that we experience for his glory and for our good. This is the work of a Good Father. Think of those times of suffering from your past: how has God used them to draw you closer to Himself, for your good, and for the good of others? What about your present sufferings and difficulties: how can you hand these over to the Father and trust that He will do the same as you journey deeper into His Heart?

_____
_____
_____
_____
_____

Earthly Fathers

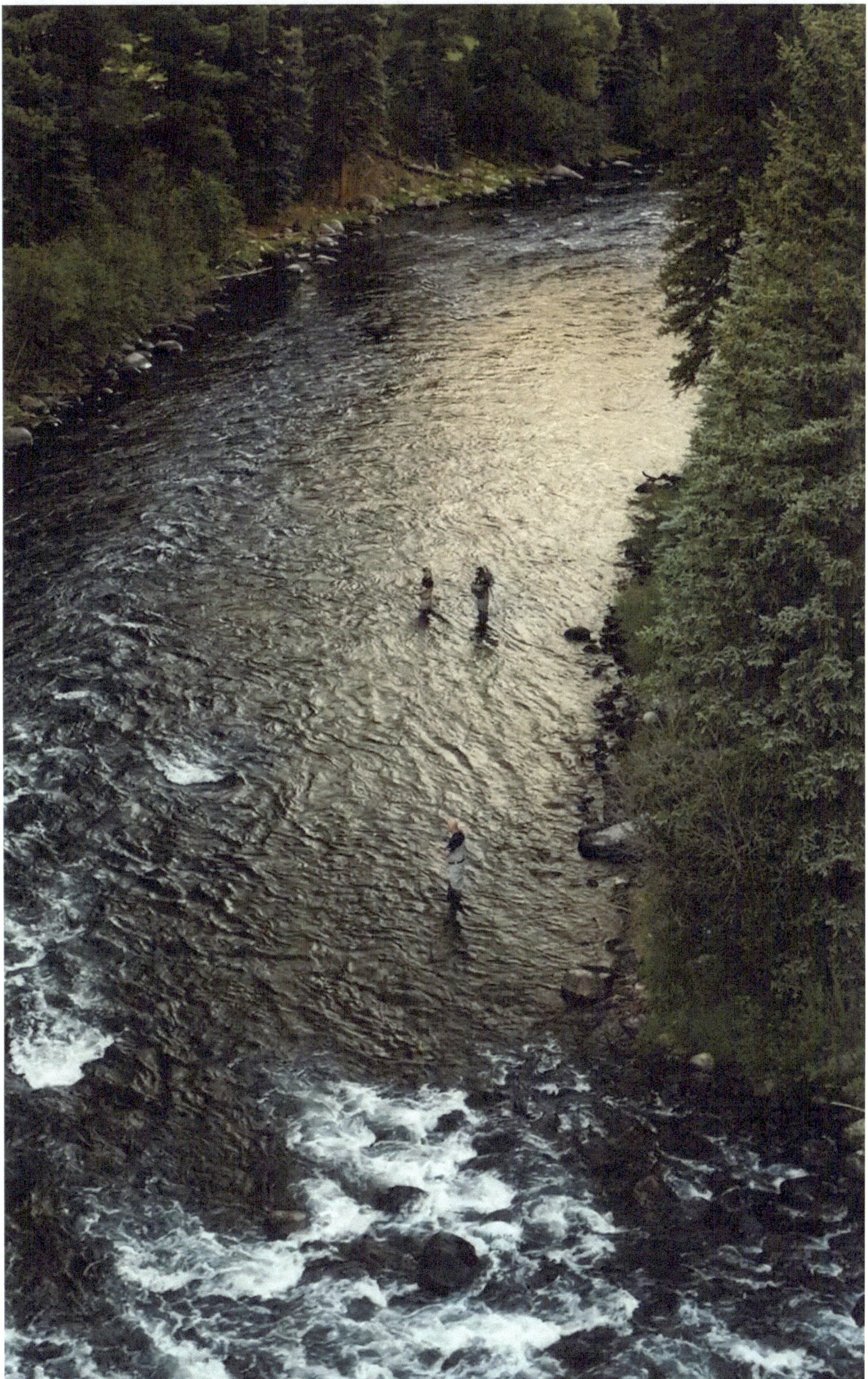

EARTHLY FATHERS
EPISODE 2

SYNOPSIS

The language of faith draws upon our human experiences and relationships. For this reason, our understanding of and relationship with God as Father begins with our relationship with our earthly fathers. In many ways, who we perceive God to be, whether true or false, begins in the home, and is formed most especially by our relationship with our fathers. God, however, is Father to us in a way that no person can be.

"Even if my father and mother forsake me, the Lord will take me in."

- Psalm 27:10 -

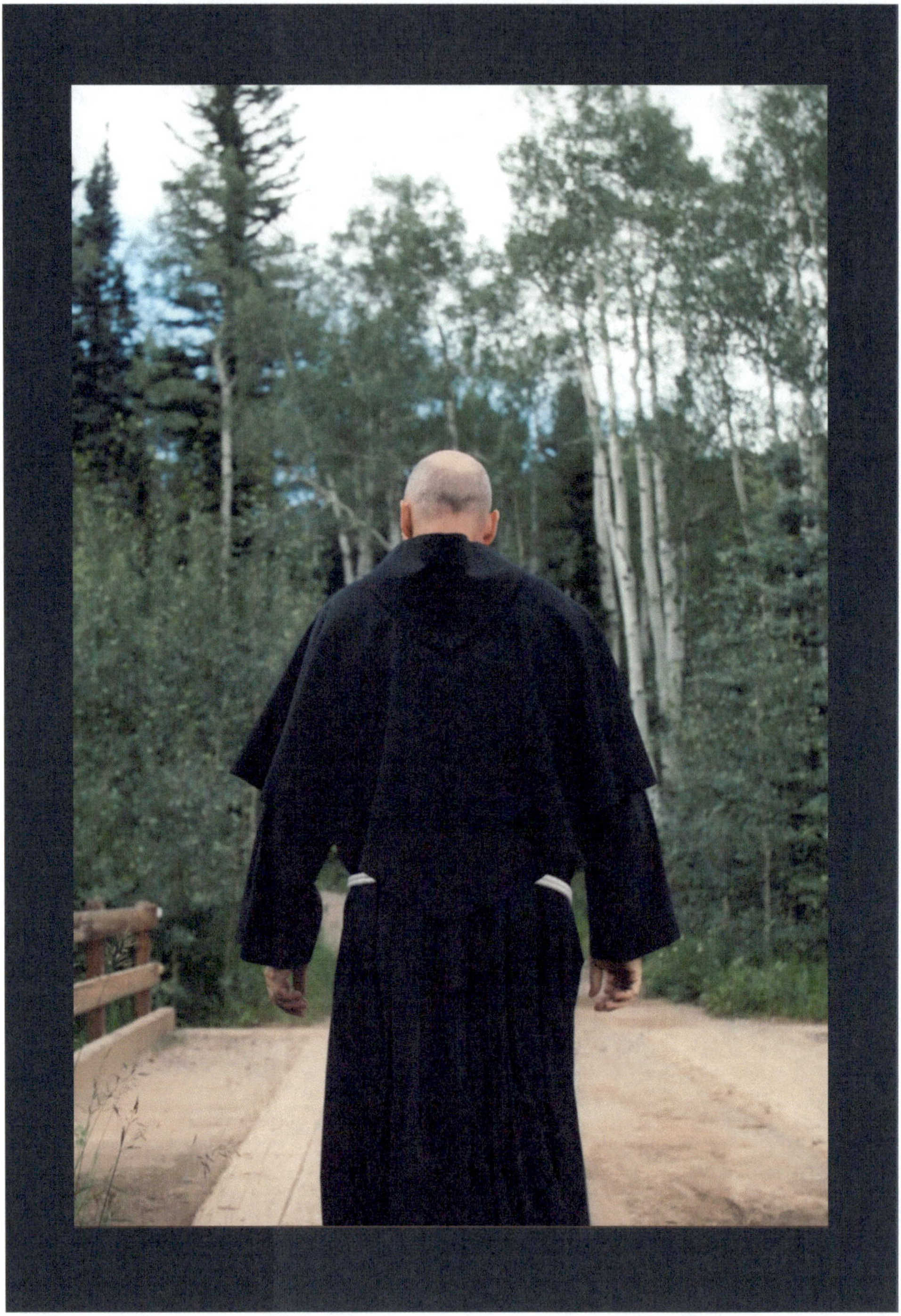

KEY TEXTS

"Father of the fatherless, defender of widows – this is the God whose abode is holy / Who gives a home to the forsaken, who leads prisoners out to prosperity..." Psalm 68:6-7

SAINTS

St. Catherine of Siena: "Everything comes from love, all is ordained for the salvation of man, God does nothing without this goal in mind."

St. Augustine: "You have made us for yourself, O Lord, and our heart is restless until it rests in You."

St. Thomas Aquinas: "wherefore, by way of excellence, piety designates the worship of God, even as God, by way of excellence, is called 'Our Father.'"

SCRIPTURE

Ephesians 1:3-6: "Blessed be the God and Father of our Lord Jesus Christ, who has blessed us in Christ with every spiritual blessing in the heavens, as he chose us in him, before the foundation of the world, to be holy and without blemish before him. In love he destined us for adoption to himself through Jesus Christ, in accord with the favor of his will, for the praise of the glory of his grace that he granted us in the beloved."

Romans 8:28: "We know that all things work for good for those who love God, who are called according to his purpose."

OTHER

Pope Benedict XVI: "God is a Father who never abandons his children..."

CCC 239: "The language of faith thus draws on the human experience of parents, who are in a way the first representatives of God for man. But this experience also tells us that human parents are fallible and can disfigure the face of fatherhood and motherhood."

GK Chesterton: "God chooses ordinary men for fatherhood to accomplish His extraordinary plan."

"Jesus revealed that God is Father in an unheard-of sense: he is Father not only in being Creator; he is eternally Father in relation to his only Son, who is eternally Son only in relation to his Father: 'No one knows the Son except the Father, and no one knows the Father'"

CCC 240

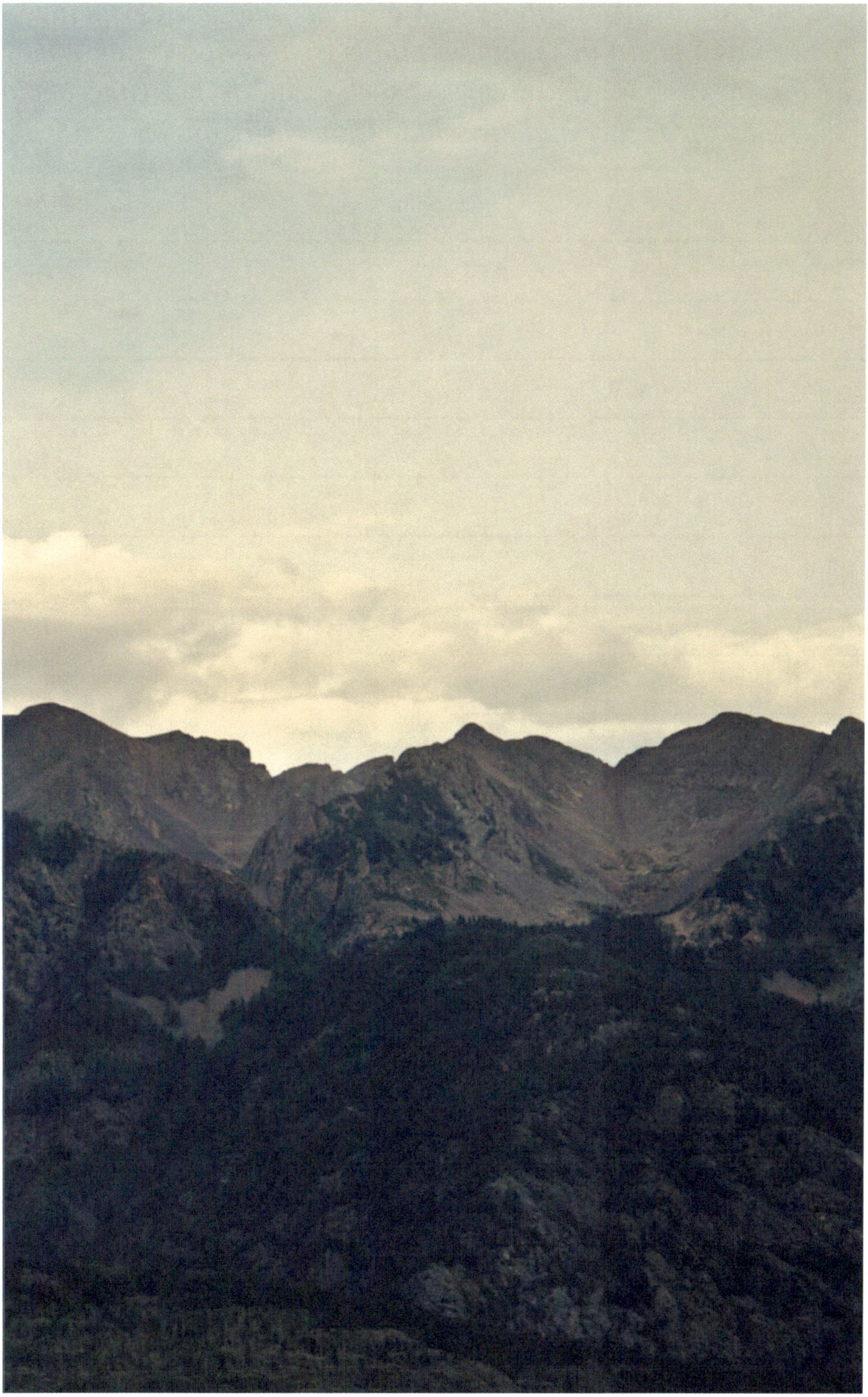

1. Can you recall a memory of your father that brings you joy? What was it about this moment that is loving or peaceful? What can this memory (or the absence of such memories) teach us about God the Father and the relationship He desires for us?

_____
_____
_____
_____
_____
_____
_____
_____
_____
_____
_____
_____
_____
_____
_____
_____
_____
_____

2. *How has your relationship with your earthly father, both for better and for worse, impacted your image of God the Father? What about that image is false and needs correction or healing? What about that image is true and needs not only validation, but gratitude?*

_____
_____
_____
_____
_____
_____
_____

3. What particular, meaning specific, actions can you take today to show those closest to you that you love them? On the other hand, who is it that needs to hear from you audibly that you love them? Ask the Holy Spirit to speak truth into this reflection.

_____
_____
_____
_____
_____
_____
_____
_____
_____
_____
_____
_____
_____
_____
_____
_____
_____
_____
_____

"God our Father, make us really alive by giving us the light to know You, the only true God, and Jesus Christ Whom You have sent. Grant us the Holy Spirit and enable us to speak volumes about Your ineffable mysteries."

Pause for Prayer

PRAYER BY SERAPION OF THMUIS

GOING

Heather Khym points out that we generally believe that God can do great things because He is God. He can move mountains, heal the blind and the sick, and even conquer death through the Resurrection. However, we falsely believe that there are parts of our lives that are untouchable and unhealable by God, and that we simply have to live with them. What are the lies about yourself that you've accepted as true in a permanent way? How can you accept that God can do great things not just generally, but specifically in and for you as well?

_____
_____
_____
_____
_____
_____
_____
_____

DEEPER

We often pray for God to help us, but we often don't realize that He may use others as a means to do so. This means that, likely on a daily basis, God desires to use you for the healing of others, for, as Dr. Breuninger stated, we can be sources of profound healing. Are you open to being God's instrument of healing and peace, or are you closed off, dwelling on yourself, your feelings, your needs, and your desires?

_____
_____
_____
_____
_____
_____
_____
_____
_____
_____
_____
_____

Chris Stefanick quoted the Catechism, which says that "The commandment to worship the Lord alone integrates man and saves him from an endless disintegration." In what ways do the little idols in our lives reflect the fact that we do not trust in the Love of God the Father?

"There's an incompleteness that Our Heavenly Father builds into everyone's experience of fatherhood so that we seek the perfection of fatherhood in Him."
- Chris Stefanick -

General Audience
May 23, 2012

REFLECTION BY POPE BENEDICT XVI

Christianity is not a religion of fear but of trust and of love for the Father who loves us. Both these crucial affirmations speak to us of the sending forth and reception of the Holy Spirit, the gift of the Risen One which makes us sons in Christ, the Only-Begotten Son, and places us in a filial relationship with God, a relationship of deep trust, like that of children; a filial relationship like that of Jesus...The Holy Spirit is the precious and necessary gift that makes us children of God, that brings about that adoption as sons to which all human beings are called...

Perhaps people today fail to perceive the beauty, greatness and profound consolation contained in the word "father" with which we can turn to God in prayer because today the father figure is often not sufficiently present and all too often is not sufficiently positive in daily life. The father's absence, the problem of a father who is not present in a child's life, is a serious problem of our time. It therefore becomes difficult to understand what it means to say that God is really our Father. From Jesus himself, from his filial relationship with God,

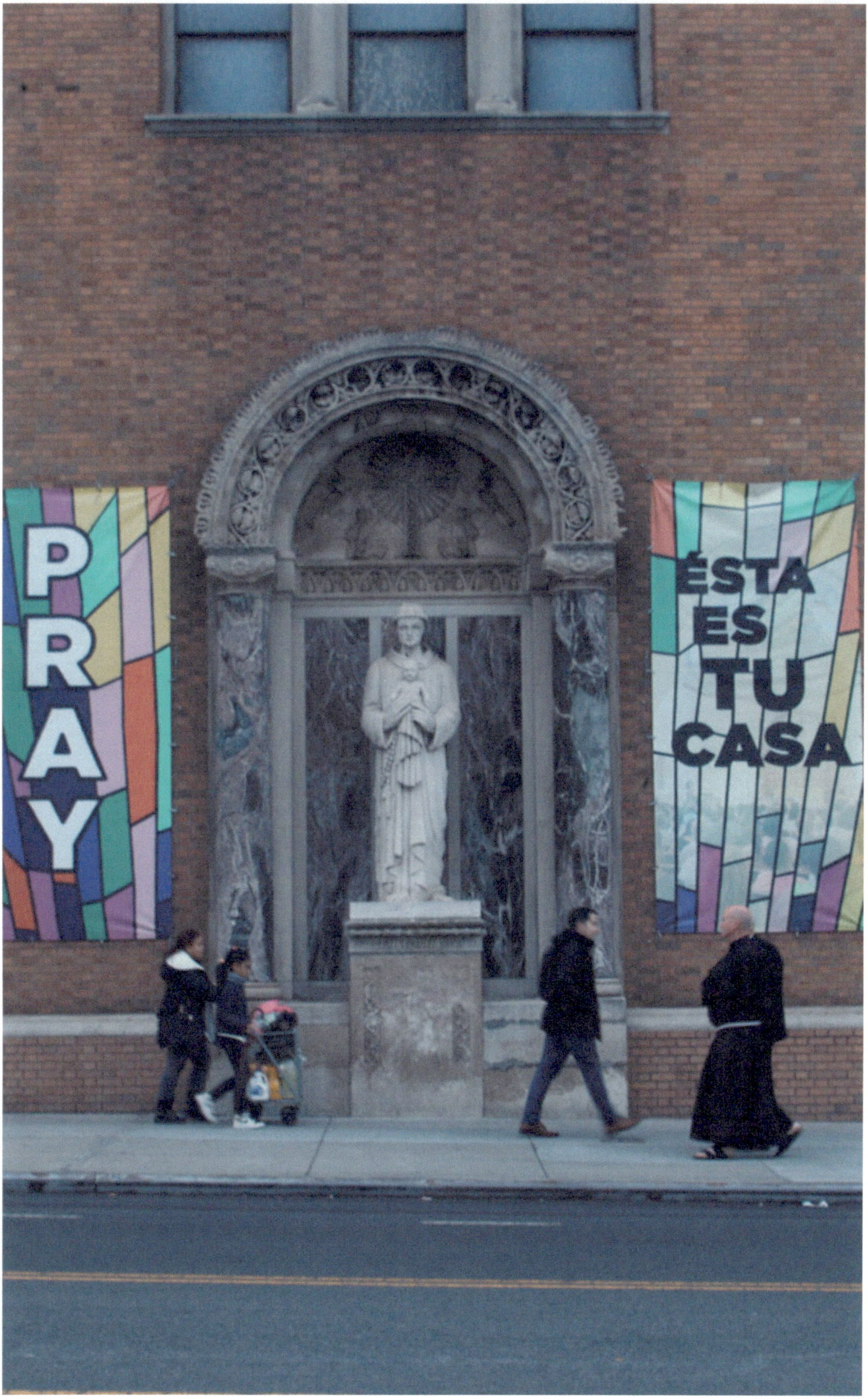
PRAY
ÉSTA ES TU CASA

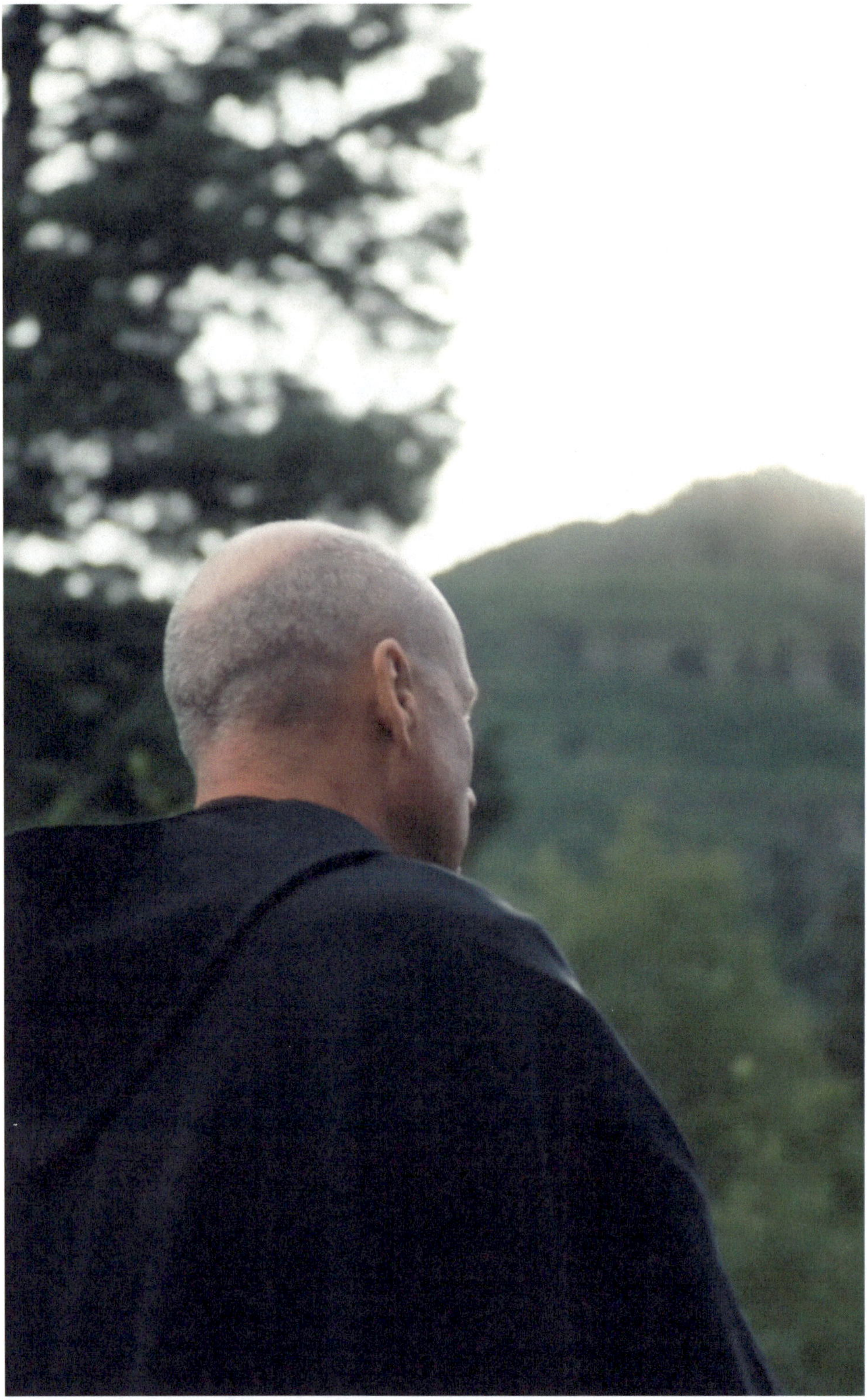

we can learn what "father" really means and what is the true nature of the Father who is in heaven.

...Christ shows us who is the father and as he is a true father we can understand true fatherhood and even learn true fatherhood... It is the very love of Jesus, the Only-Begotten Son — who goes even to the point of giving himself on the Cross — that reveals to us the true nature of the Father: he is Love and in our prayers as children we too enter this circuit of love, the love of God that purifies our desires....

...Jesus in his turn accepts us in his humanity and even in his being Son, so that we too may enter into his specific belonging to God. Of course, our being children of God does not have the fullness of Jesus. We must increasingly become so throughout the journey of our Christian existence, developing in the following of Christ and in communion with him so as to enter ever more intimately into the relationship of love with God the Father which sustains our life.

It is this fundamental reality that is disclosed to us when we open ourselves to the Holy Spirit and he makes us turn to God saying "Abba!", Father.

REFLECT

Come, Holy Spirit. In a world of lies and brokenness, truth and goodness need validation. Take a moment now to remind yourself of the truth of who God is as Father and Creator. Then, take a moment to recall the goodness of God in His Providence and Mercy.

SENDING FORTH

Ask God to place on your heart a spirit of thanksgiving. For many, this spirit is difficult to accept, but for all, it is lacking in some way. Take a moment, then, to thank God for those relationships you have been fortunate to be a part of that have taught you the truth of who God is. Then, go a bit further: how can you be the instrument by which God wishes to form those around you? What can God teach others by your example of faith?

Sons and Daughters

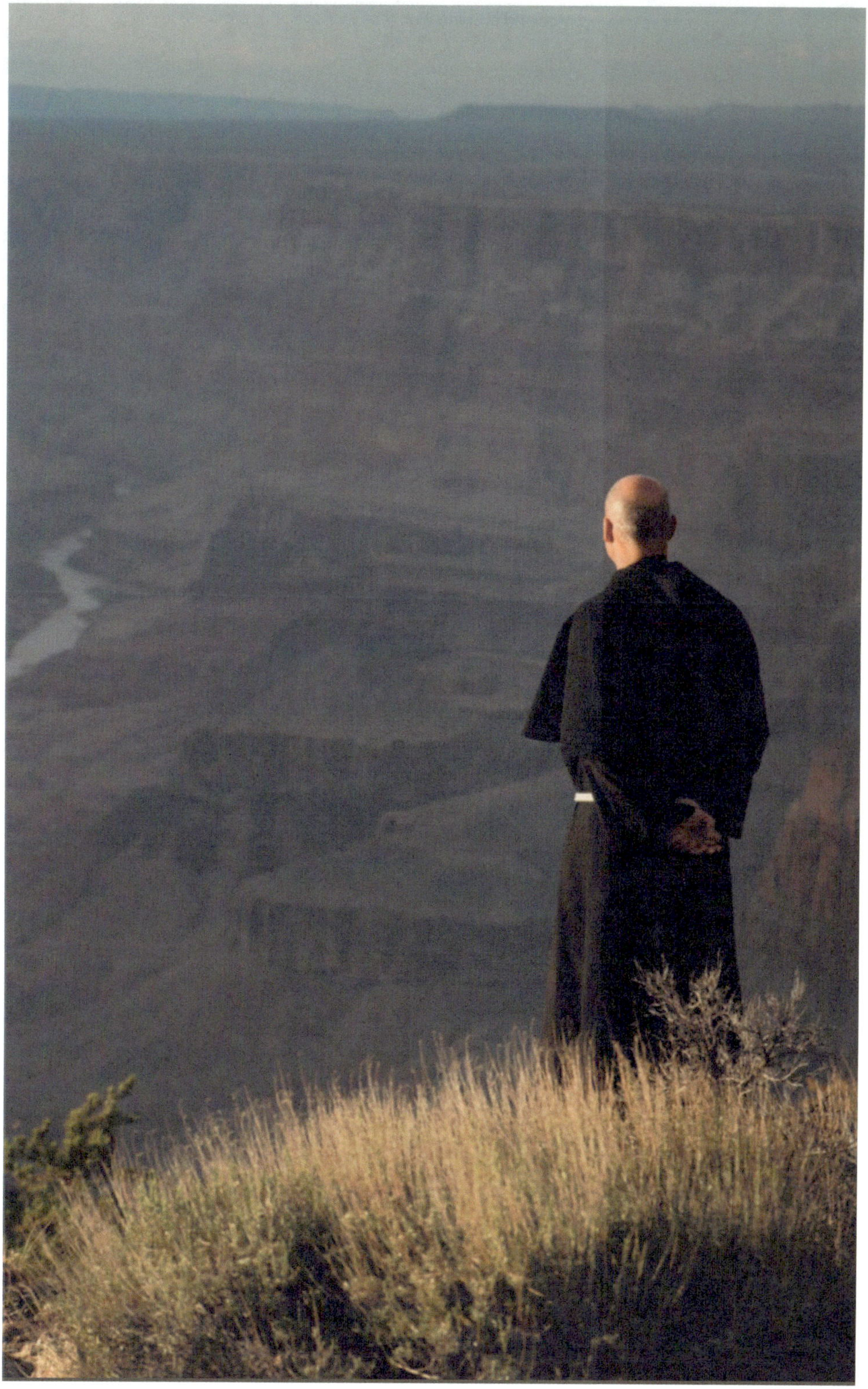

SONS & DAUGHTERS
EPISODE 3

SYNOPSIS

Each of us is a son or a daughter of God. This is the root of our identity. Unfortunately, we live in an age that questions more than ever the nature of the identity of the human person. However, we are not the sum of our failures or sins, and our identities are not up to us. Instead, as the Scriptures say, we are sons and daughters first and foremost; in that, God sees us with a gaze of love. We then must imitate Christ's Sonship and grow in what it means to be a good son or a good daughter not only of God the Father, but also of our earthly parents as well.

"Remember, of these parents you were born; what can you give them for all they gave you?"

- Sirach 7:28 -

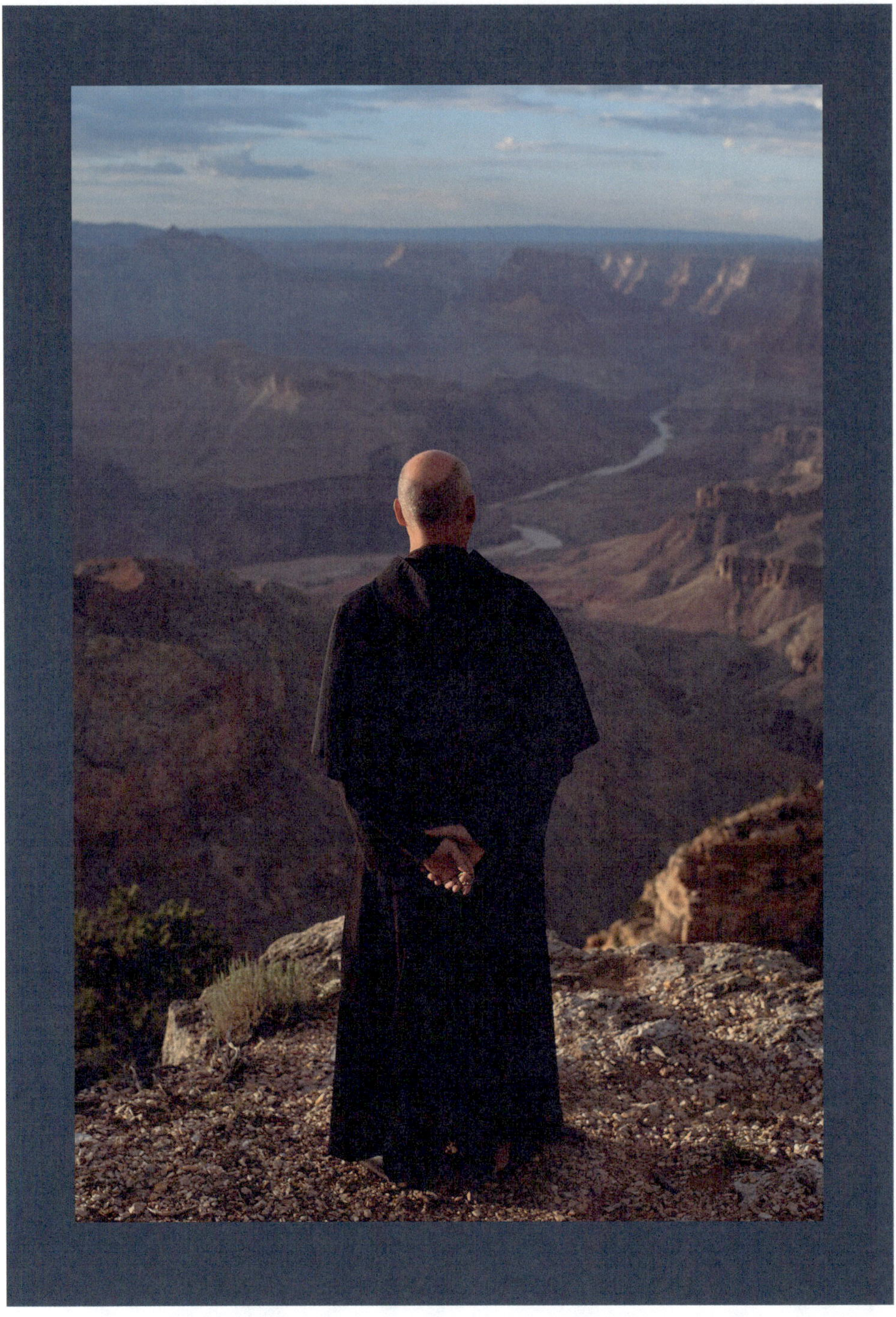

KEY TEXTS

"But when the fullness of time had come, God sent his Son, born of a woman, born under the law, to ransom those under the law, so that we might receive adoption." Galatians 4:4-5

SAINTS

St. Francis of Assisi: "I am who I am in the eyes of God, nothing more and nothing less"

Mother Teresa: "By blood, I am Albanian. By citizenship, I am Indian. By faith, I am a Catholic nun. As to my calling, I belong to the world. As to my heart, I belong entirely to the heart of Jesus."

St. John Cardinal Henry Newman: "Therefore, I will trust Him...He does nothing in vain. He knows what He is about."

SCRIPTURE

Matthew 3:16-17: "After Jesus was baptized, he came up from the water and behold, the heavens were opened [for him], and he saw the Spirit of God descending like a dove [and] coming upon him. And a voice came from the heavens, saying, 'This is my beloved Son, with whom I am well pleased.'"

John 5:19: "Jesus answered and said to them, 'Amen, amen, I say to you, a son cannot do anything on his own, but only what he sees his father doing; for what he does, his son will do also.'"

OTHER

Pope Francis: "Every distinction becomes secondary to the dignity of being children of God, who, through his love, creates a real and substantial equality."

CCC 2214: "The divine fatherhood is the source of human fatherhood; this is the foundation of the honor owed to parents. The respect of children, whether minors or adults, for their father and mother is nourished by the natural affection born of the bond uniting them. It is required by God's commandment."

"See what love the Father has bestowed on us that we may be called the children of God. Yet so we are. The reason the world does not know us is that it did not know him. Beloved, we are God's children now..."

1 John 3:1-2

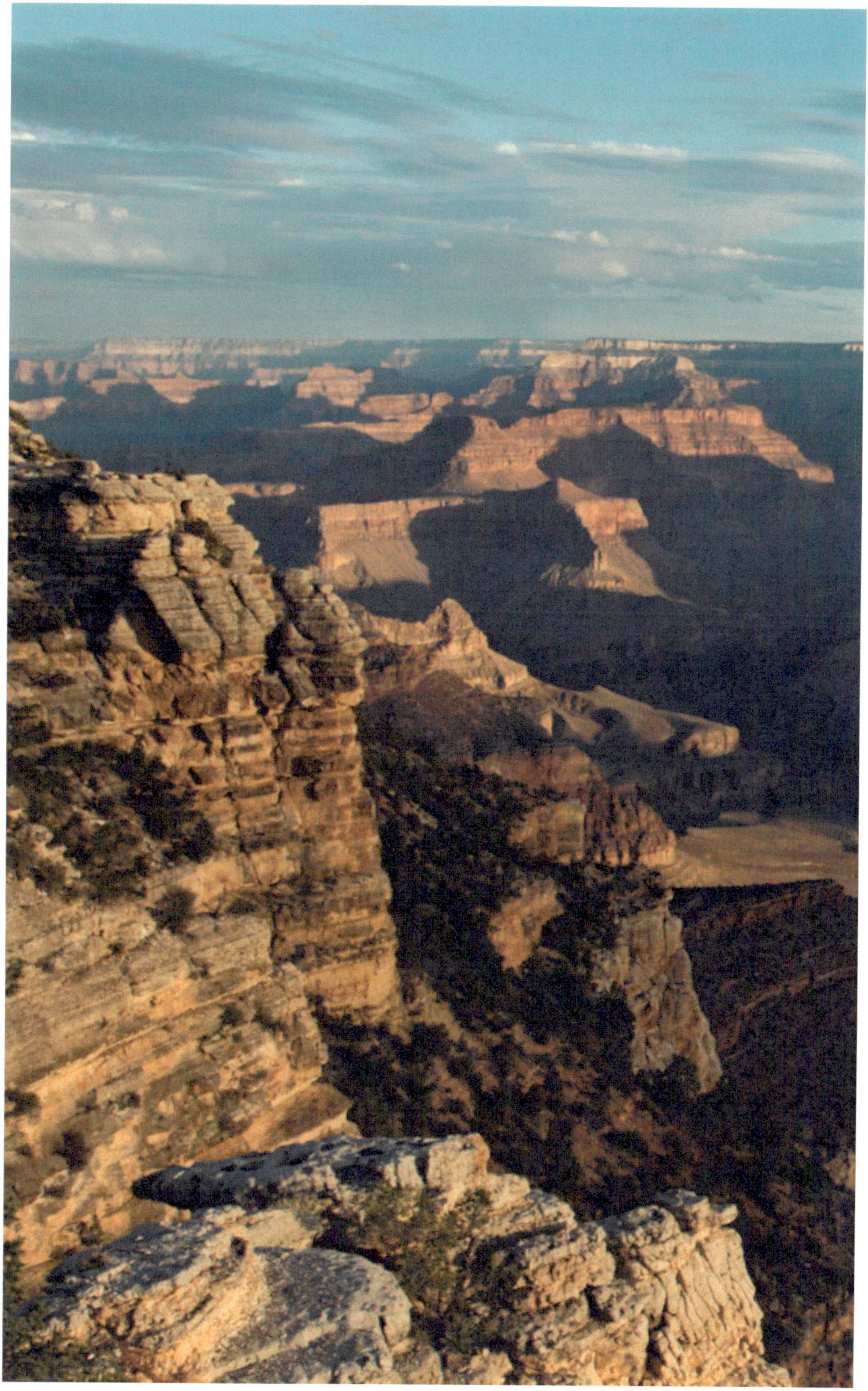

1. If you're a parent, how can you place your children into the hands of God the Father? What steps can you take to reconcile your children to both you and God, no matter their age, by way of apology, prayer, or honest conversation?

2. Romans 8:17 says that we are "heirs of God and joint heirs with Christ," and the very first paragraph of the Catechism speaks of being "heirs" of God's "blessed life." Do you think of this inheritance as merely being something to come later, after death? What might it mean to be an heir of God's blessed life now?

3. Where you lack God, you lack freedom. Where you lack God, you lack peace. Where you lack God, you lack joy. Where do you, as a son or daughter of the Good Father, need to lean into God's Providence to experience the fullness of these gifts?

"God our Father, make us really alive by giving us the light to know You, the only true God, and Jesus Christ Whom You have sent. Grant us the Holy Spirit and enable us to speak volumes about Your ineffable mysteries."

Pause *for* Prayer

PRAYER BY SERAPION OF THMUIS

GOING

Dr. Bergsma and Heather Khym spoke of the necessity to be claimed, especially as children. Is your heart vulnerable enough and humble enough, like that of a child, to be claimed by the Father, or in pride do you act more from the position that you are your own foundation?

DEEPER

Katie Hartfiel revealed that there was a time when she felt like giving up praying for her father, but Jesus showed her an image of him holding up an umbrella, blocking His grace. Who is it in your life that you have given up on, that you believe to be too far gone? How might the Spirit be moving you to pray and fast for this person?

Bishop Espaillat spoke of the human person as the Imago Dei, the Image of God. Is that what people first see when they see you? Is that what people first think when they think about you? Or, is your identity wrapped up in a different, more worldly reputation?

"Stop trying to find yourself and find Him...you need to find the One who created you in His Image and Likeness."
- Bishop Joseph Espaillat -

REFLECTION BY SAINT TERESA OF CALCUTTA

National Prayer Breakfast Speech
February 3, 1994

This is the meaning of true love, to give until it hurts.

I can never forget the experience I had in visiting a home where they kept all these old parents of sons and daughters who had just put them into an institution and forgotten them…I saw that in that home these old people had everything–good food, comfortable place, television, everything, but everyone was looking toward the door. And I did not see a single one with a smile on the face. I turned to the Sister and I asked: "Why do these people, who have every–every comfort here, they are there looking toward the door? Why are they not smiling? I am so used to seeing the smiles on our people, even the dying ones smile." And Sister said: "This is the way it is nearly everyday. They are expecting–they are hoping that a son or a daughter will come to visit them. They are hurt because they are forgotten."

And see, this neglect to love brings spiritual poverty. Maybe in our own family we have somebody who is feeling lonely, who is feeling

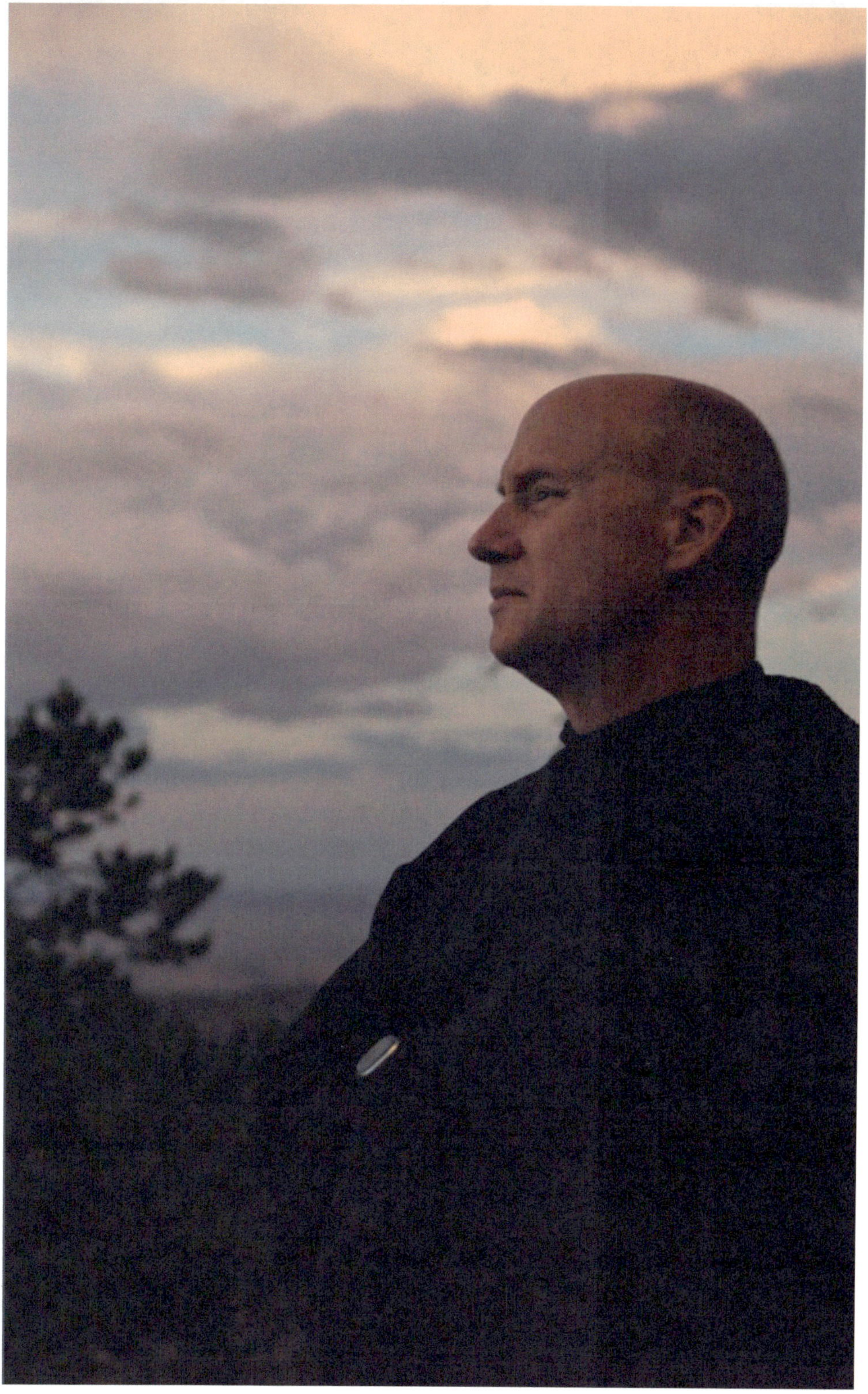

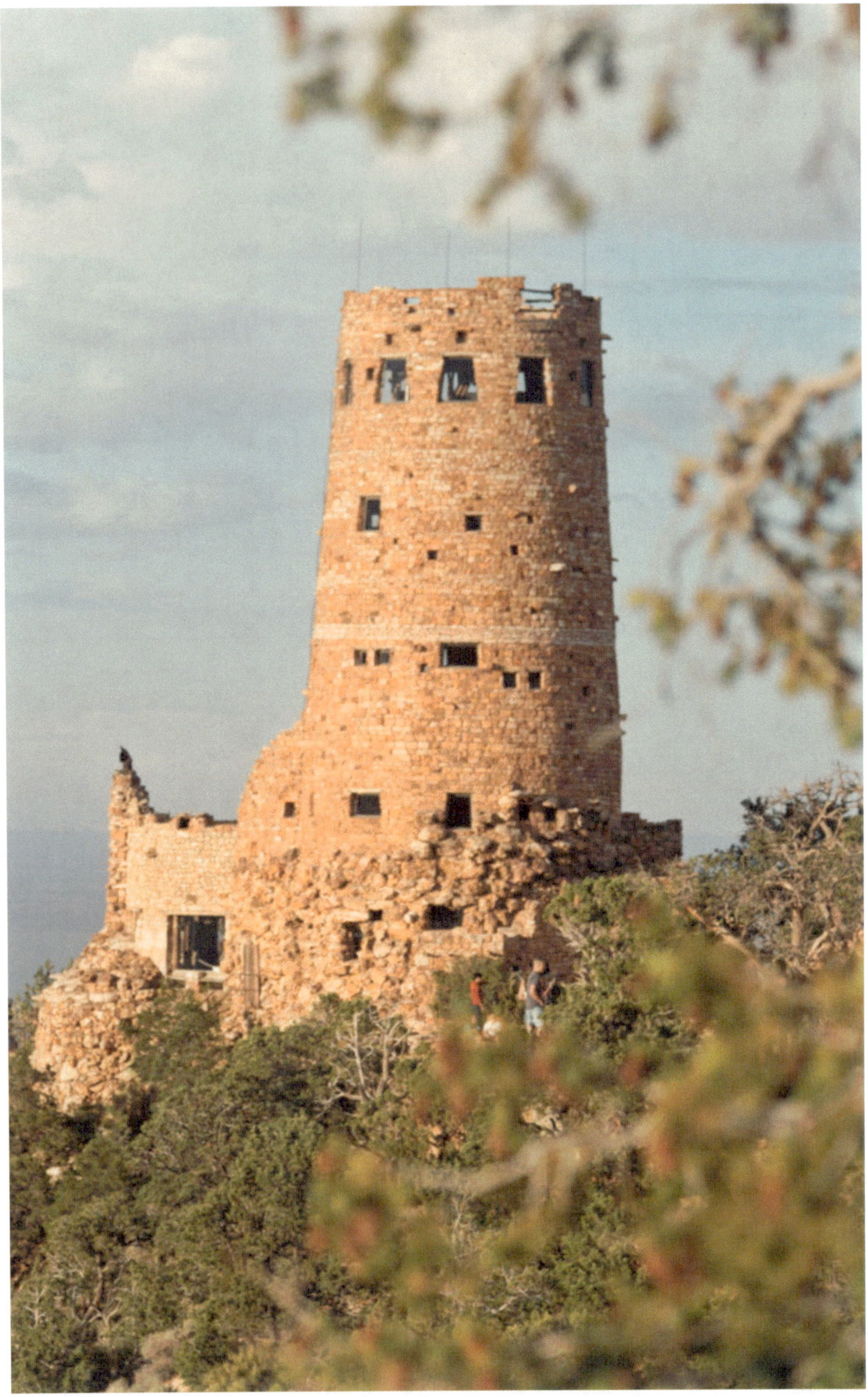

REFLECTION BY SAINT TERESA OF CALCUTTA

sick, who is feeling worried. Are we there? Are we willing to give until it hurts in order to be with our family, or do we put our interests first? These are the questions we must ask ourselves, especially as we begin this year of the family. We must remember that love begins at home. And we must also remember that the future of humanity passes through the family...

If we are contemplatives in the heart of the world with all its problems, these problems can never...discourage us. We must always remember that God tells us in Scripture: "Even if a mother could forget the child in her womb"–something impossible, but even if she could forget–"I will never forget you."

And so, here I am talking with you. I want you to find the poor here, right in your own home first. And begin love there. Be that good news to your own people first...

...this is where love begins–at home in the family.

REFLECT

Come, Holy Spirit. Forgiveness is always possible, even if it is not always received. If there is someone you need to forgive, whether a parent, other family member, or someone else, find time to do so in the sight of God. It may not come with the feelings you think ought to be there, but as a choice of the will, God knows it to be authentic. Then, pray for guidance from the Holy Spirit in that relationship.

SENDING FORTH

Both at the Baptism in the Jordan and the Transfiguration, God the Father delights in His Son. Surely Our Lord, in His humanity, delighted also in being a Son of the Father. Have you taken delight in this role, in this identity? Knowing that faith does not stem from feelings, can you choose to accept this truth, even if you feel dryness there?

A Holy Family

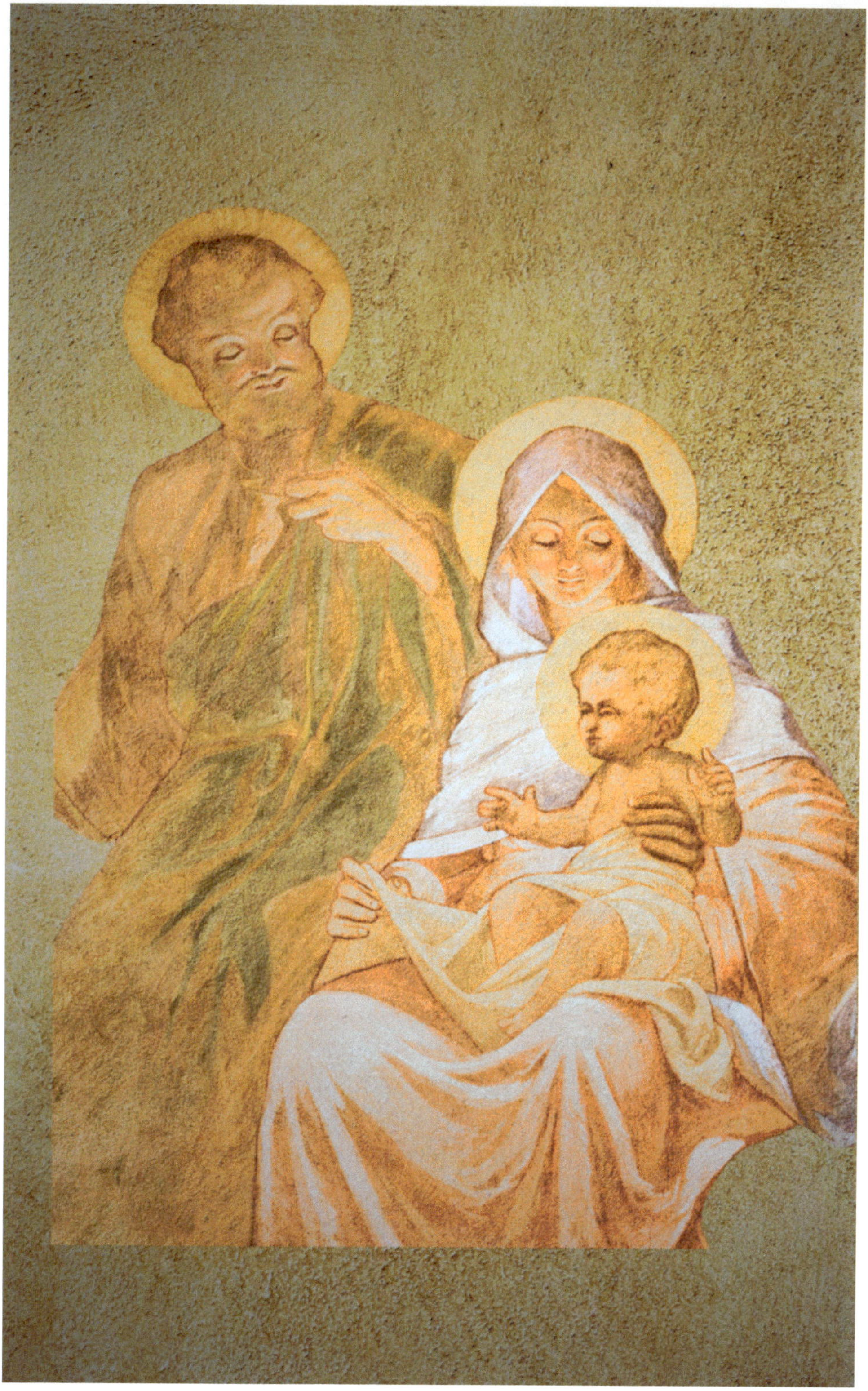

A HOLY FAMILY
EPISODE 4

SYNOPSIS

Mothers and fathers both play a role in the life of a person, and to that end God has given us exemplary examples of both. First of these is Mary, who became the Mother of all Christians by her Son's words to she and John at the foot of the Cross. Our Blessed Mother holds us in her heart, intercedes for us, and gives us an example of pure faith, hope, and love. Secondly there is St. Joseph, the earthly father and protector of Jesus, who is a model of fatherhood by his courage and docility to the promptings of the Spirit.

"We know well that the Blessed Virgin is the Queen of heaven and earth, but she is more mother than queen!"

- St. Thérèse -

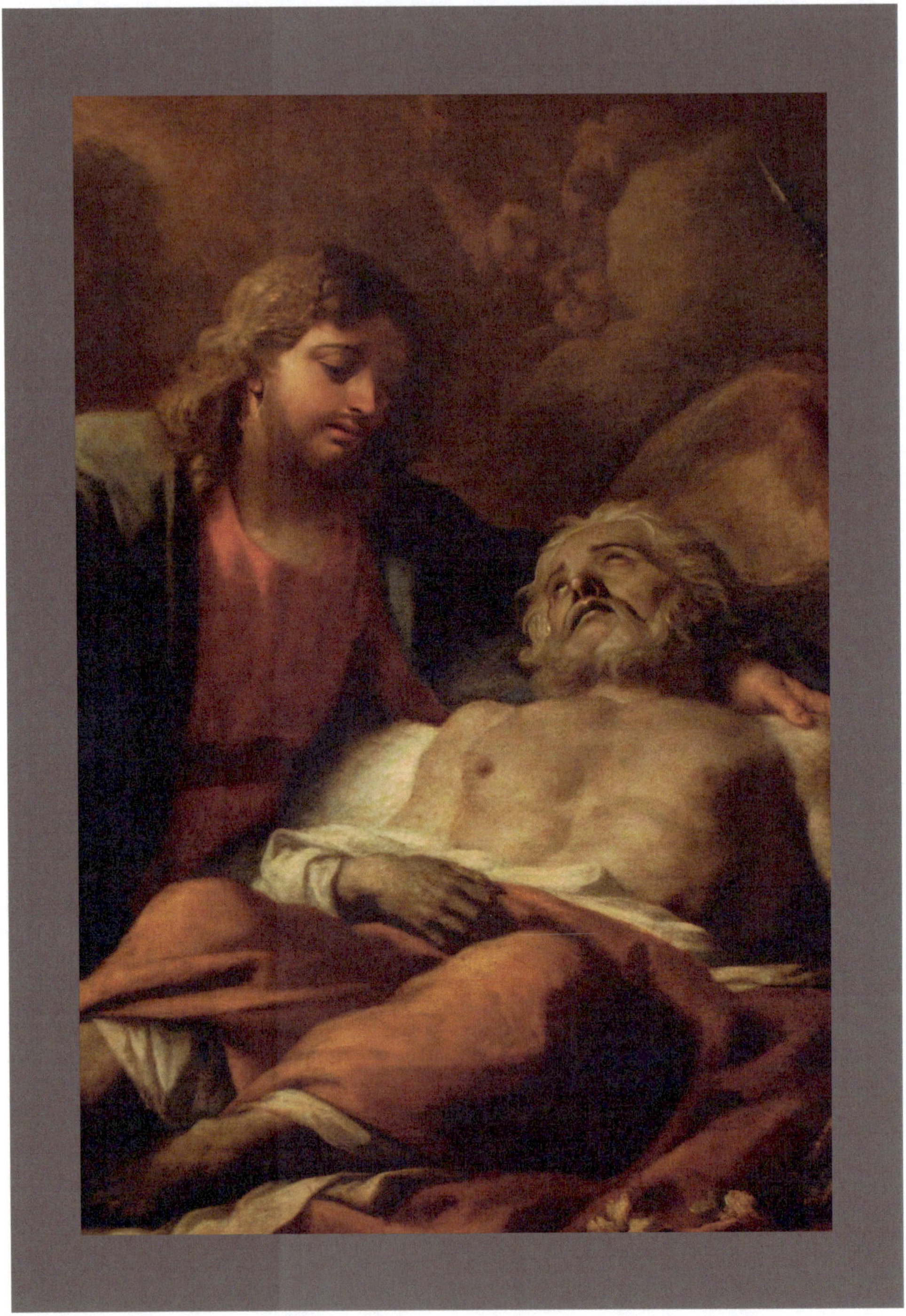

KEY TEXTS

"Mary said, 'Behold, I am the handmaid of the Lord. May it be done to me according to your word.' Then the angel departed from her." Luke 1:38

SAINTS

St. Thérèse: "You love us, Mary, as Jesus loved us, and for us you accept being separated from Him. To love is to give everything. It's to give oneself... Refuge of sinners, He leaves us to you when He leaves the Cross to wait for us in Heaven."

St. Thomas Aquinas: "Some saints are privileged to extend to us their patronage with particular efficacy in certain needs, but not in others; but our holy patron St. Joseph has the power to assist us in all cases, in every necessity, in every undertaking."

SCRIPTURE

John 19:26-27: "When Jesus saw his mother and the disciple there whom he loved, he said to his mother, 'Woman, behold, your son.' Then he said to the disciple, 'Behold, your mother.' And from that hour the disciple took her into his home."

Matthew 23:37: "Jerusalem, Jerusalem... how many times I yearned to gather your children together, as a hen gathers her young under her wings, but you were unwilling!"

Isaiah 66:13: "As a mother comforts her son, so will I comfort you."

OTHER

Pope Francis: "In his relationship to Jesus, Joseph was the earthly shadow of the heavenly Father: he watched over him and protected him, never leaving him to go his own way."

Lumen Gentium 53: "The Virgin Mary, who at the message of the angel received the Word of God in her heart and in her body and gave Life to the world, is acknowledged and honored as being truly the Mother of God...Because of this gift of sublime grace she far surpasses all creatures, both in heaven and on earth."

"[T]he Holy Family...enables us to appreciate the gift of family intimacy in a special way, and spurs us to offer human warmth... in those unfortunately numerous situations which, for various reasons, lack peace, harmony, in a word, lack 'family.'"

Pope Saint John Paul II

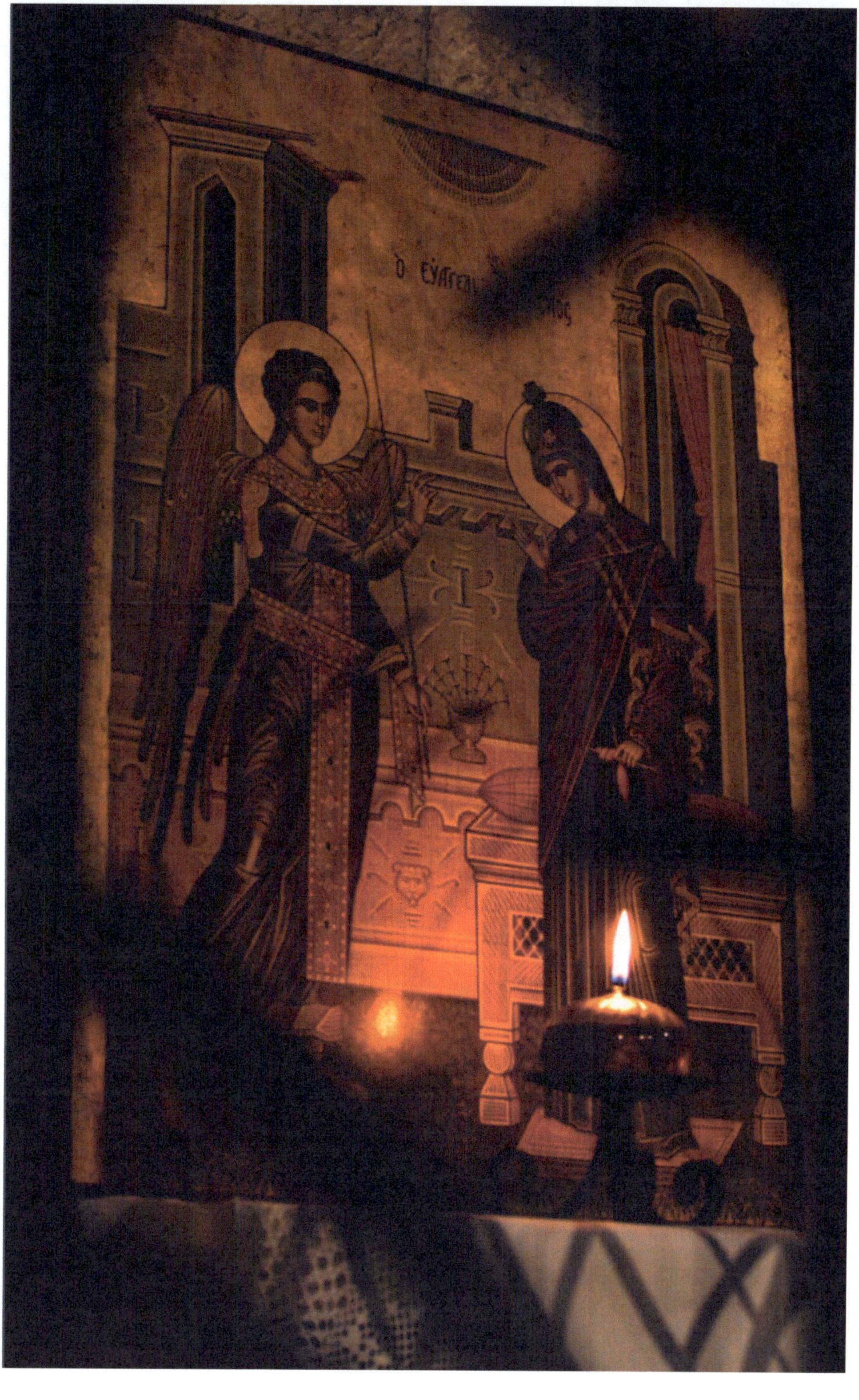

1. Though they had different roles in salvation history, Mary and Joseph shared this in common: docility to the Holy Spirit. How can your role as son, daughter, father, mother, or other relation be strengthened by embracing this same docility?

_____

_____

_____

_____

_____

_____

_____

_____

_____

_____

_____

_____

_____

_____

_____

_____

_____

2. In Matthew's Gospel, Jesus speaks of his desire to gather his people "as a hen gathers her young under her wings" (Matthew 23:37). However, Jesus also says that they were unwilling. In what corners of your life do you run from God or pridefully believe that you can do it alone?

3. The situation of the Holy Family was, in the eyes of the world, something of a scandal, yet Joseph justly and courageously took Mary into his home. In what particular ways are you overly concerned about what others think of you? Do you consider what other people might think before submitting your will on a daily basis to God the Father?

_____
_____
_____
_____
_____
_____
_____
_____
_____
_____
_____
_____
_____
_____
_____
_____

"God our Father, make us really alive by giving us the light to know You, the only true God, and Jesus Christ Whom You have sent. Grant us the Holy Spirit and enable us to speak volumes about Your ineffable mysteries."

Pause for Prayer

PRAYER BY SERAPION OF THMUIS

GOING

Heather Khym says that Mary is strong and tender, but not passive. She and her Son at all times infused their authority and influence with love, so how can you do so in your relationships, especially those in which you have authority? How can that help you to find a balance between being, on the one hand, too nice or loose, and, on the other hand, controlling or overbearing?

DEEPER

Katie Hartfiel speaks to the necessity of having a community with which to share hardships. Are there areas of your life in which you are trying to suffer through on your own? At a minimum, how can you further lean on the members of the Holy Family as a model, and are there others that you could be leaning on as well (friends, small groups, etc.) but are reluctant to do so?

Dr. Bergsma reflected on the spiritual union of the New Adam (Jesus) and the New Eve (Mary), and how John, then, became the first son of the Church. These words: 'life,' 'unity,' 'children,' 'mother,' etc...do they still denote to you merely biological realities? Why is it important to lean into the spiritual, deeper, and fuller meanings of these words?

_____
_____
_____
_____
_____
_____
_____
_____
_____
_____
_____
_____
_____
_____
_____
_____

"God espouses Himself to His bride, which is His people, in order to bring forth new life, and the image, the one person who so perfectly represents that fertile bride, is the Blessed Mother."
- Dr. John Bergsma -

Redemptoris Mater

REFLECTION BY POPE SAINT JOHN PAUL II

Of the essence of motherhood is the fact that it concerns the person. Motherhood always establishes a unique and unrepeatable relationship between two people: between mother and child and between child and mother. Even when the same woman is the mother of many children, her personal relationship with each one of them is of the very essence of motherhood. For each child is generated in a unique and unrepeatable way, and this is true both for the mother and for the child. Each child is surrounded in the same way by that maternal love on which are based the child's development and coming to maturity as a human being...

...Mary's motherhood, which becomes man's inheritance, is a gift: a gift which Christ himself makes personally to every individual. The Redeemer entrusts Mary to John because he entrusts John to Mary. At the foot of the Cross there begins that special entrusting of humanity to the Mother of Christ...

The Marian dimension of the life of a disciple of Christ is expressed in a special way precisely

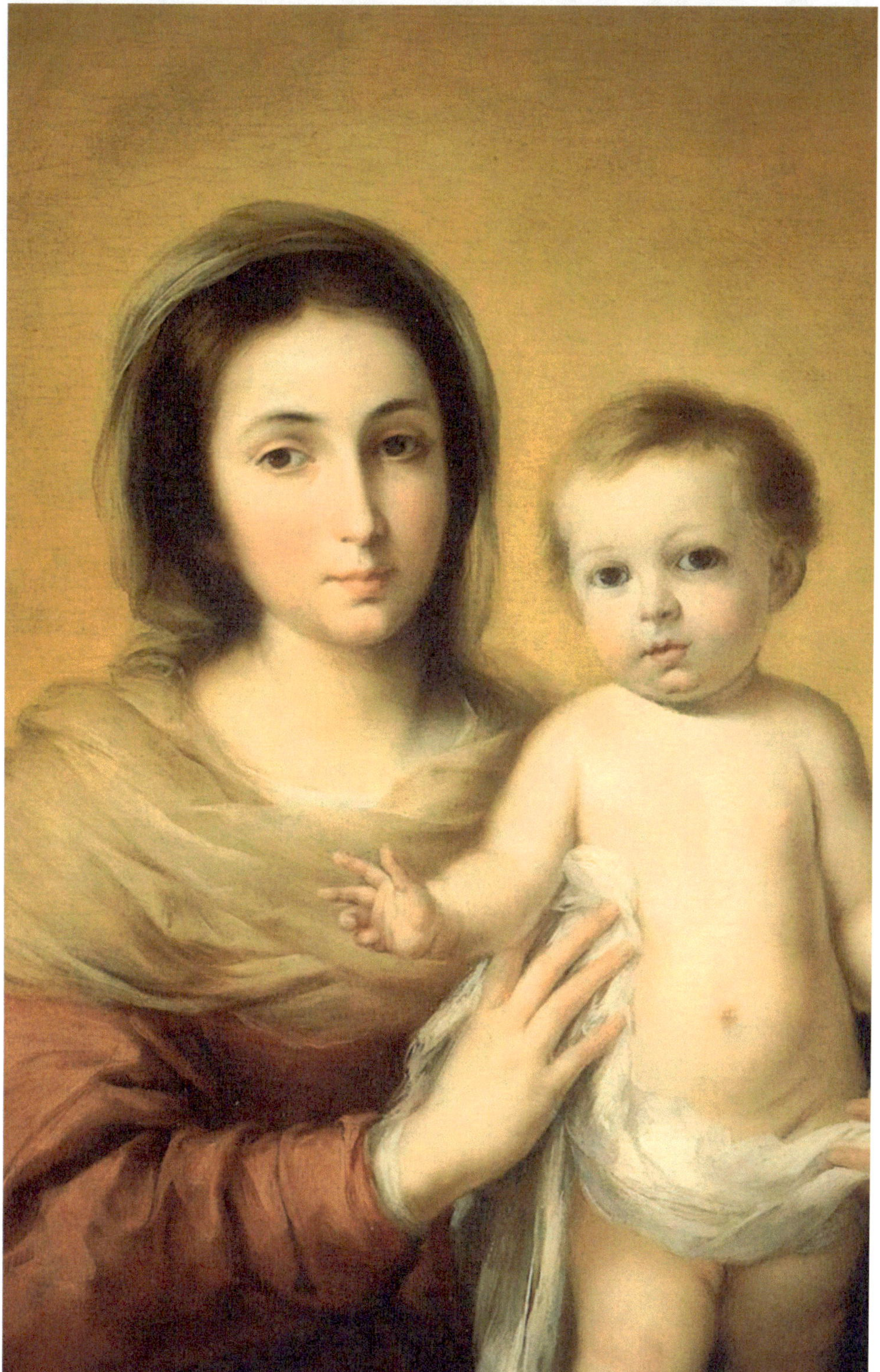

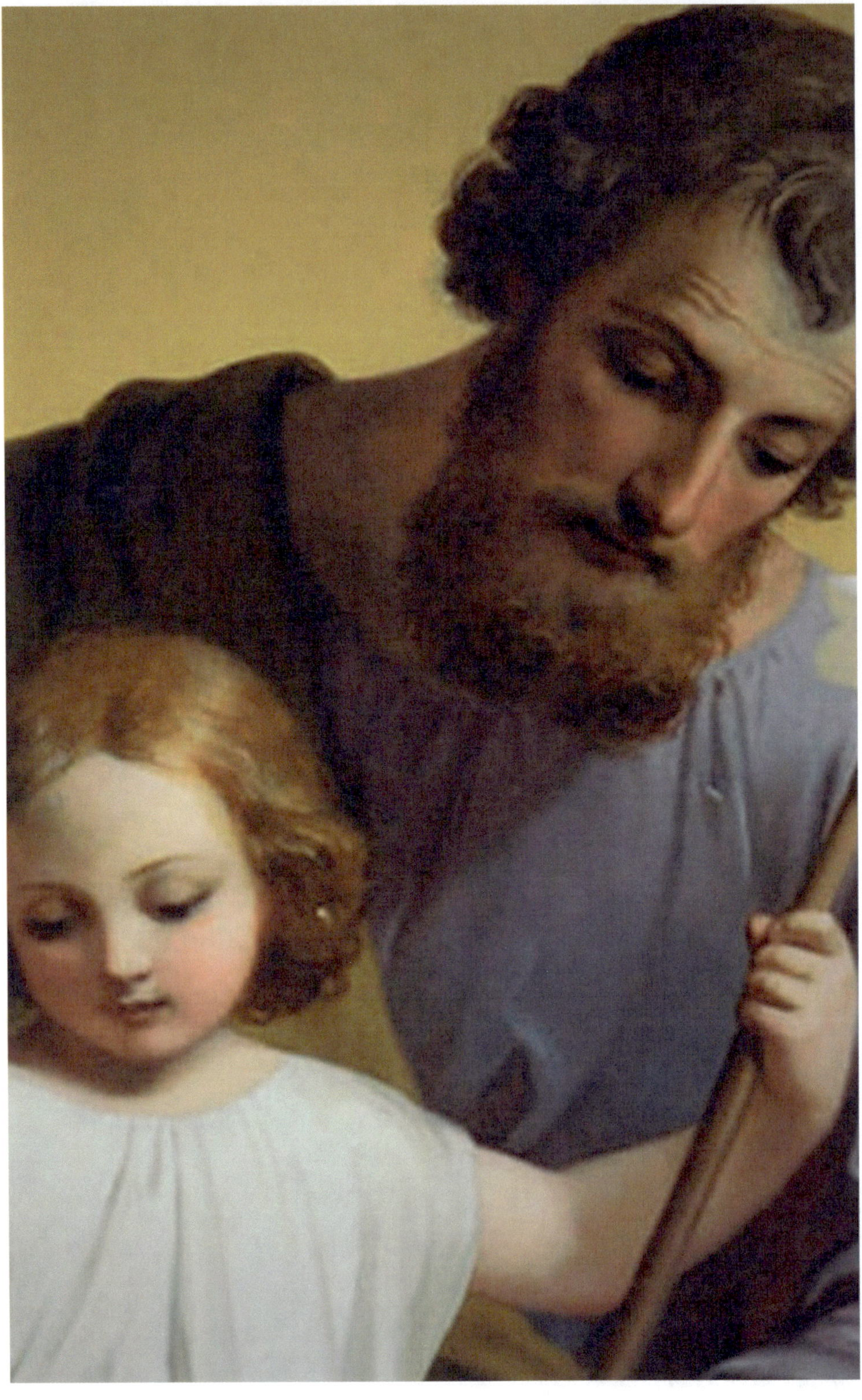

REFLECTION BY POPE SAINT JOHN PAUL II

through this filial entrusting to the Mother of Christ, which began with the testament of the Redeemer on Golgotha. Entrusting himself to Mary in a filial manner, the Christian, like the Apostle John, "welcomes" the Mother of Christ "into his own home" and brings her into everything that makes up his inner life, that is to say into his human and Christian "I": he "took her to his own home." Thus the Christian seeks to be taken into that "maternal charity" with which the Redeemer's Mother "cares for the brethren of her Son," "in whose birth and development she cooperates" in the measure of the gift proper to each one through the power of Christ's Spirit...

...Mary can be said to continue to say to each individual the words which she spoke at Cana in Galilee: "Do whatever he tells you." For he, Christ, is the one Mediator between God and mankind; he is "the way, and the truth, and the life" (Jn. 14:6); it is he whom the Father has given to the world, so that man "should not perish but have eternal life" (Jn. 3:16). The Virgin of Nazareth became the first "witness" of this saving love of the Father, and she also wishes to remain its humble handmaid always and everywhere...she wishes to act upon all those who entrust themselves to her as her children.

REFLECT

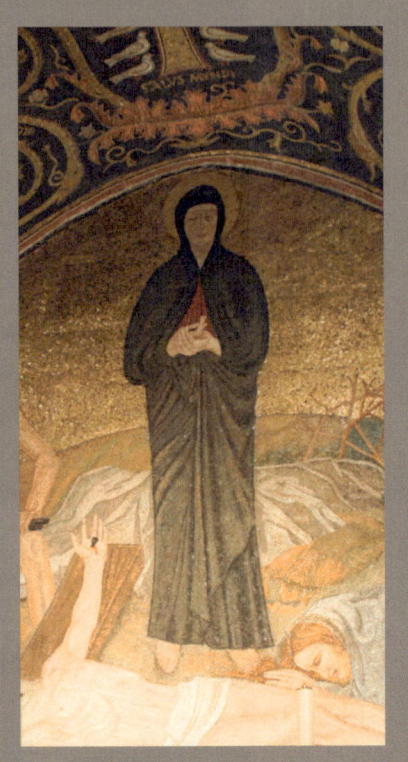

Come, Holy Spirit. At the foot of the cross, Jesus gives Mary over to the disciple John. That makes Mary in many ways the Mother of the Church, but it also certainly means that Jesus wants you to embrace Mary as a Mother as well. It is easy to get caught up in the apologetics of Mary and learning to defend her from falsehoods. But, as a result, is Mary distant to you? Take time in silence to remember how Mary holds you in her heart as a true Mother.

SENDING FORTH

Each of us has heard that we must imitate Mary in her discipleship and faithfulness, but we have not thought about what that meant for her and the Church. Her fiat to the Angel Gabriel initiated the salvation of the world, but meant that Mary would witness her Son's Crucifixion from the foot of the Cross and play an active role in the Church. Are you willing to say "yes" to God's will for you, even if you know it may change things for you or even lead to suffering? Imitate Mary's courage, humility, and faith, and ask for her intercession in this.

_____

_____

_____

_____

_____

Priestly Fatherhood

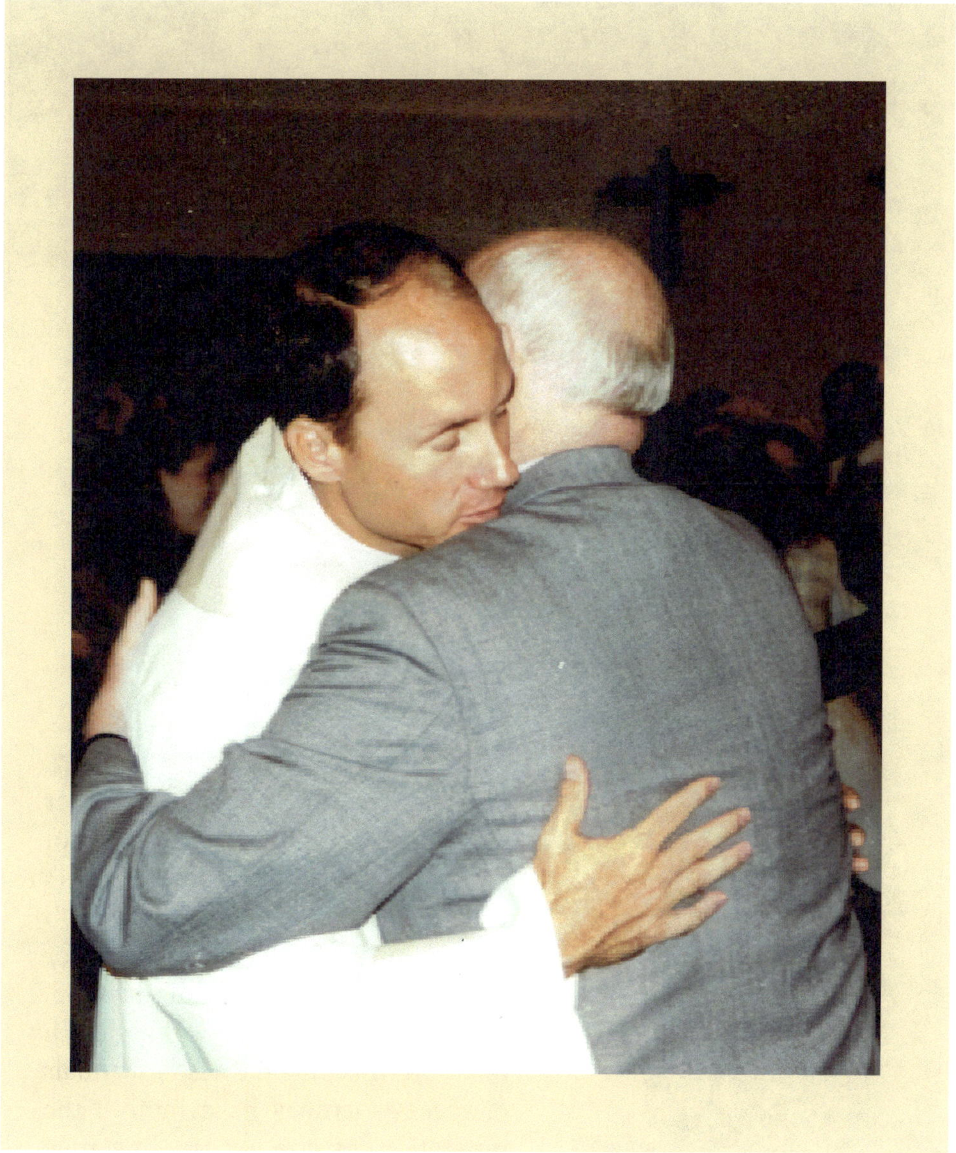

PRIESTLY FATHERHOOD
EPISODE 5

SYNOPSIS

Priests take on the role of father for spiritual children. Though not biological fathers, they model God's Fatherhood by nourishment through the sacraments, offering sacrifice for His children, leading souls to God, extending mercy, and speaking truth in all circumstances. Priestly scandals of recent memory have injured the reputation of the priest, but now more than ever the world needs loving spiritual fathers to help reveal the true Love of God the Father.

"Every high priest is taken from among men and made their representative before God, to offer gifts and sacrifices for sins."

- Hebrews 5:1 -

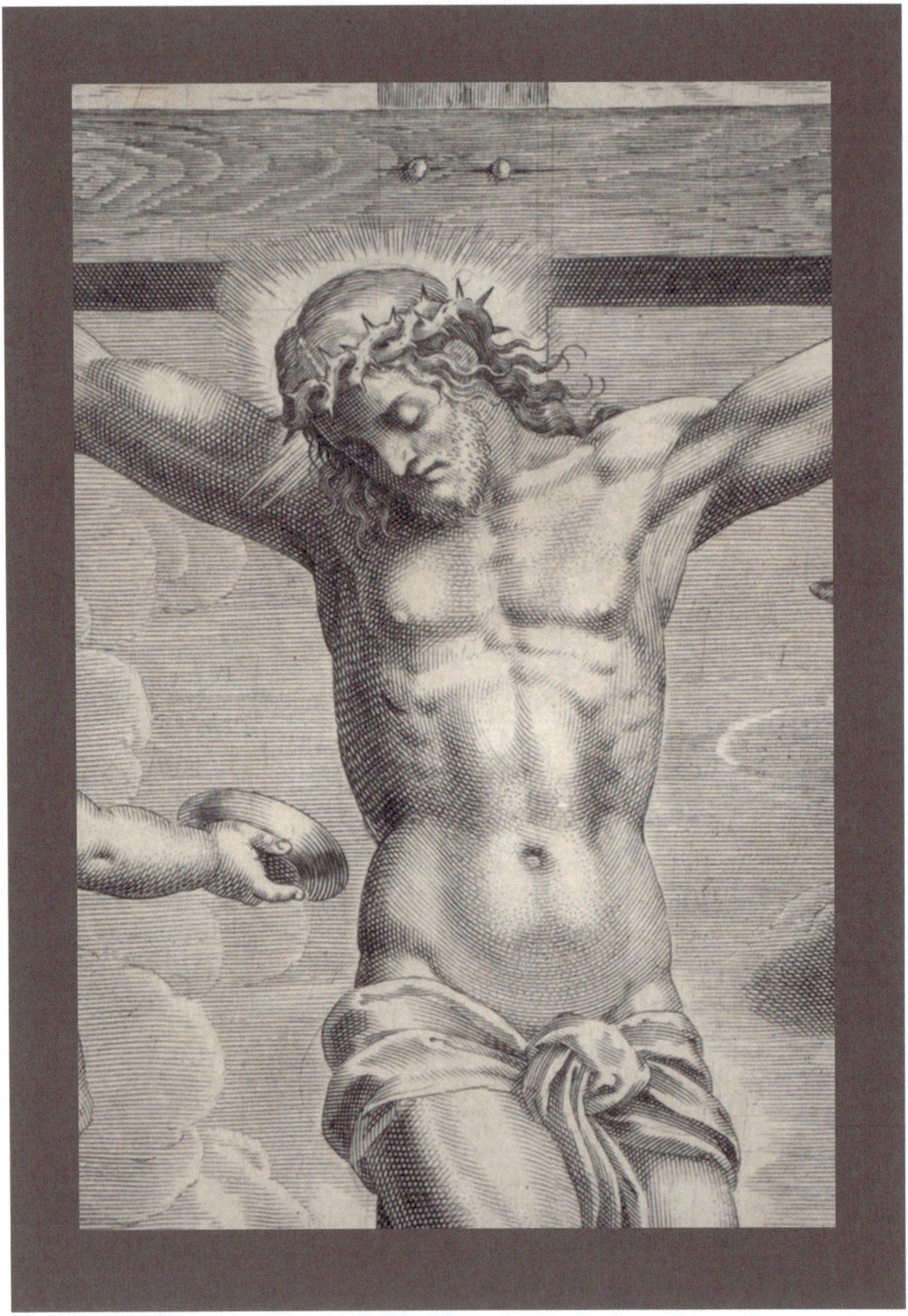

KEY TEXTS

"Even if you should have countless guides to Christ, yet you do not have many fathers, for I became your father in Christ Jesus through the gospel." 1 Corinthians 4:15

SAINTS

Pope St. Paul VI: "Modern man listens more willingly to witnesses than to teachers, and if he does listen to teachers, it is because they are witnesses."

St. Alphonsus Liguori: "...the end for which God has instituted the priesthood has been to appoint on earth public persons to watch over the honor of his divine majesty, and to procure the salvation of souls."

St. John Vianney: "The priest is not a priest for himself...he is for you."

SCRIPTURE

Hebrews 4:14-15: "Therefore, since we have a great high priest who has passed through the heavens, Jesus, the Son of God, let us hold fast to our confession. For we do not have a high priest who is unable to sympathize with our weaknesses, but one who has similarly been tested in every way, yet without sin."

Matthew 23:9: "Call no one on earth your father; you have but one Father in heaven."

Ephesians 3:14-15: "For this reason I kneel before the Father, from whom every family in heaven and on earth is named..."

OTHER

Pope Benedict XVI: "Because he belongs to Christ, the priest is radically at the service of all people: he is the minister of their salvation..."

CCC 1546: "The faithful exercise their baptismal priesthood through their participation, each according to his own vocation, in Christ's mission as priest, prophet, and king."

Presbyterorum Ordinis 15: "...the true minister of Christ works in humility trying to do what is pleasing to God."

"Yes, the priest stands at the altar... and makes a long supplication, not in order that fire from heaven may consume the things that lie in open view, but that grace, lighting on the Sacrifice, may thereby inflame the souls of all, and show them brighter than silver purified in the fire."

Saint John Chrysostom

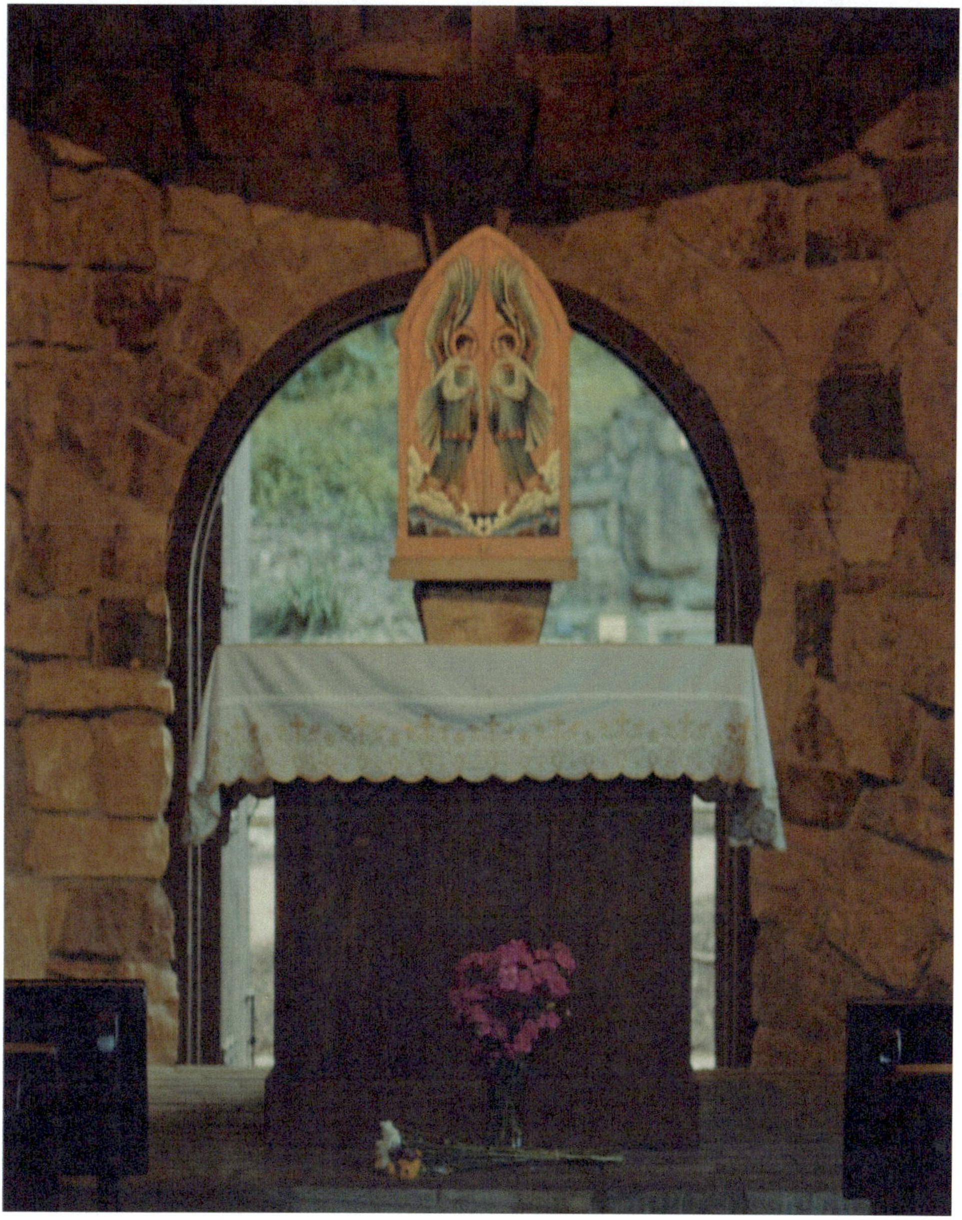

1. Every person must be anchored to God first and foremost. What are some concrete steps you can take to ensure that this is happening with those you are in closest relationship with? Are you scared to let go, or do you faithfully and over time entrust your loved ones to God's Providence?

2. Describe a circumstance in which you had to share the truth, even when it was painful. Did it bear fruit that you could see, or is this a circumstance or relationship that needs further entrusting to God the Father?

3. Who is a priest or priests that you need to express a renewed gratitude for? How can you build him up, support him in his ministry, give him what he needs, and express that gratitude for him?

"God our Father, make us really alive by giving us the light to know You, the only true God, and Jesus Christ Whom You have sent. Grant us the Holy Spirit and enable us to speak volumes about Your ineffable mysteries."

Pause for Prayer

PRAYER BY SERAPION OF THMUIS

GOING

Chris Stefanick says that fatherhood is a "posture of soul" towards the world, and the same can certainly be said of motherhood. As a man or a woman, do you assume this posture to those around you, motivated by charity, especially towards those who are more vulnerable?

DEEPER

Fr. Jacques Philippe said, in the context of his vocation story, "I felt it was better to say 'yes' to God than to say 'no.'" Is your faith and trust in God this simple? Or, do you complicate faith by overconsidering circumstances or feelings, whether those of others or those of your own?

Fr. Dave reflects on how discernment is always between two goods. This is true in large matters, but also in smaller matters also. Do you invite the Holy Spirit into your decisions of discernment, large and small, or do you rely merely on your own intuitions? Is it even possible to know God's will in such a decision without calling upon Him?

"It's important, I think, that we understand that discernment is always between two goods; it's not between a good and a bad."
- Fr. Dave Pivonka, TOR -

Homily
Apil 13, 1973

[M]en become priests of their own free will, because they want to, and this is a very supernatural reason. They know that they are not renouncing anything in the normal sense of the word. Through their vocation…they have been devoted to the service of the Church and of all souls. This full, divine vocation led them to sanctify their work, to sanctify themselves in their work, and to seek the sanctification of others in the context of their professional relationships.

As Christian faithful, priests and lay people share one and the same condition, for God our Lord has called us to the fullness of charity which is holiness…

There is no such thing as second-class holiness. Either we put up a constant fight to stay in the grace of God and imitate Christ, our Model, or we desert in that divine battle. God invites everyone; each person can become holy in his own state in life…

Here we have the priest's identity: he is a direct and daily instrument of the saving grace which

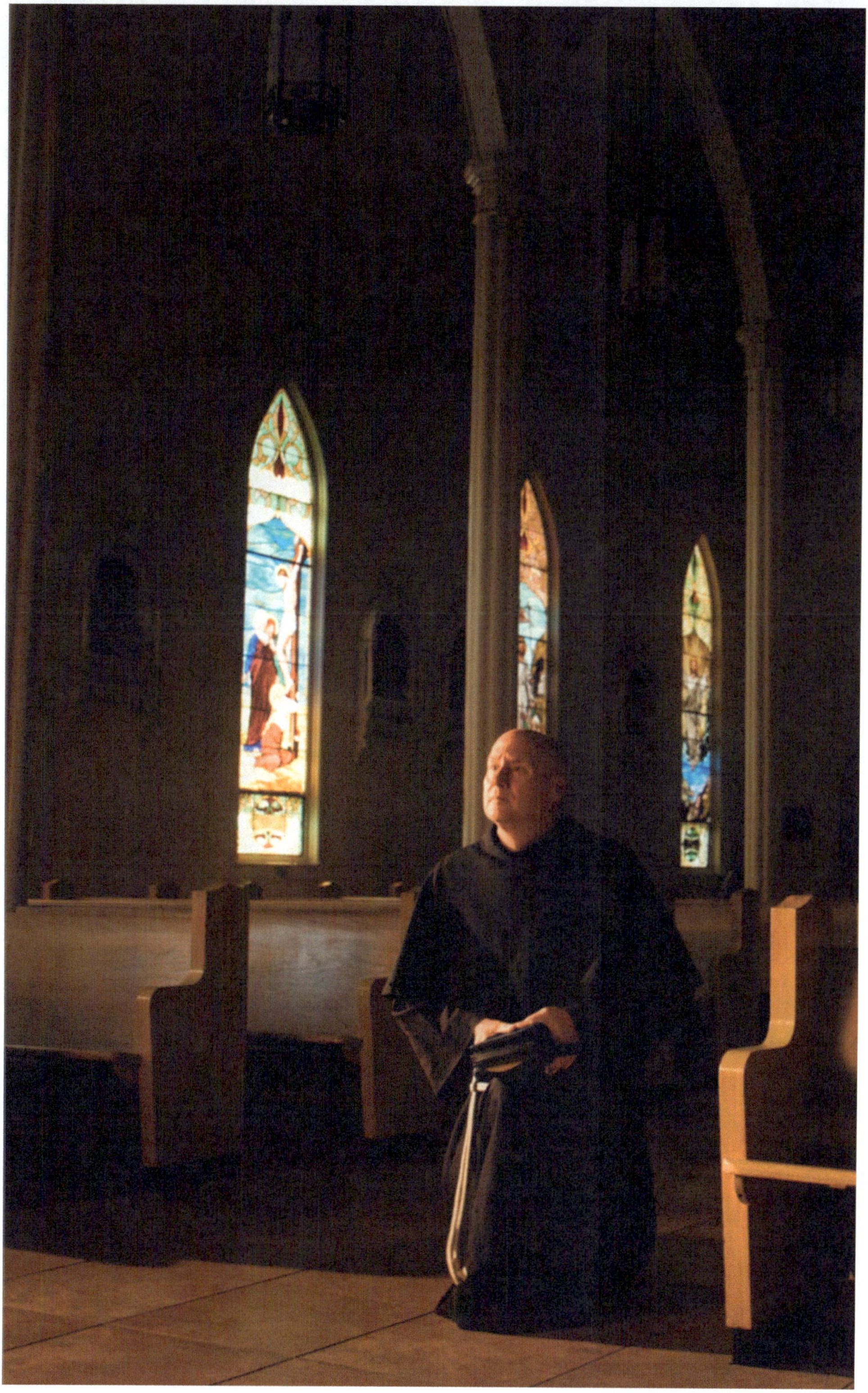

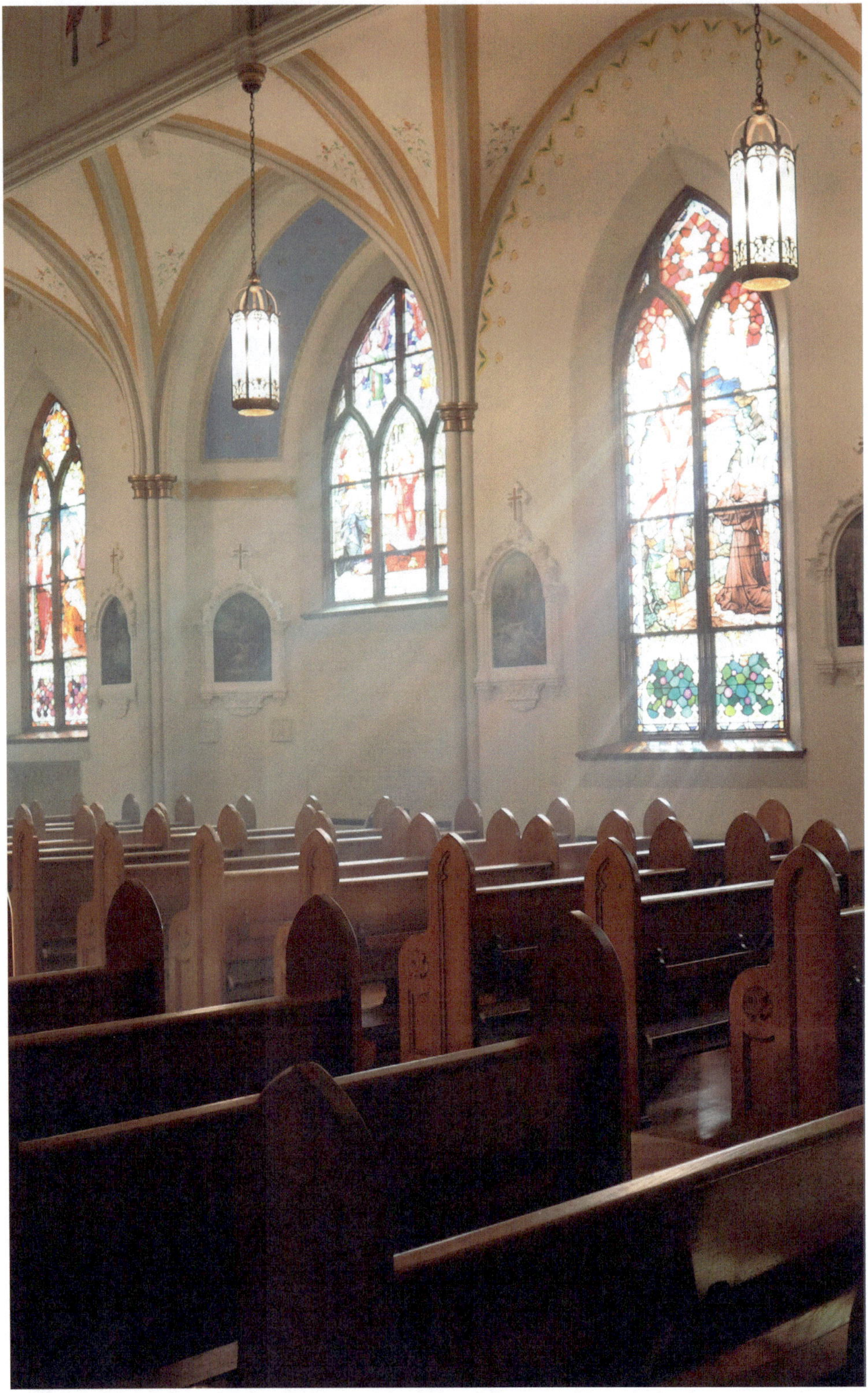

REFLECTION BY SAINT JOSEMARÍA ESCRIVÁ

Christ has won for us. If you grasp this, if you meditate on it in the active silence of prayer, how could you ever think of the priesthood in terms of renunciation? It is a gain, an incalculable gain….

The genuine Christian priesthood has not disappeared from God's Church. The teaching which we have received from the divine lips of Jesus has not changed. There are many thousands of priests throughout the world who really do respond to their vocation, quietly, undramatically. They have not fallen into the temptation to throw overboard a treasure of holiness and grace which has existed in the Church from the very beginning.

It warms my heart to think of the quiet human and supernatural dignity of those brothers of mine, scattered throughout the world. It is only right that they should now feel themselves surrounded by the friendship, help and affection of many Christians. And when the moment comes for them to enter God's presence, Jesus will go out to meet them. He will glorify forever those who have acted on earth in his Person and in his name. He will shower them with that grace of which they have been ministers.

REFLECT

Come, Holy Spirit. God begets, creates, or gives life through his Word, not a biological act. Whether or not you are a biological parent, do your words, in the imitation of God's creative and loving power, create life in others? Are our words motivated by charity? Or, alternatively, are we seeking to build ourselves up through pride or tearing others down? Spend some time steeped in the Word of God, the Scriptures, and allow God to beget life within you.

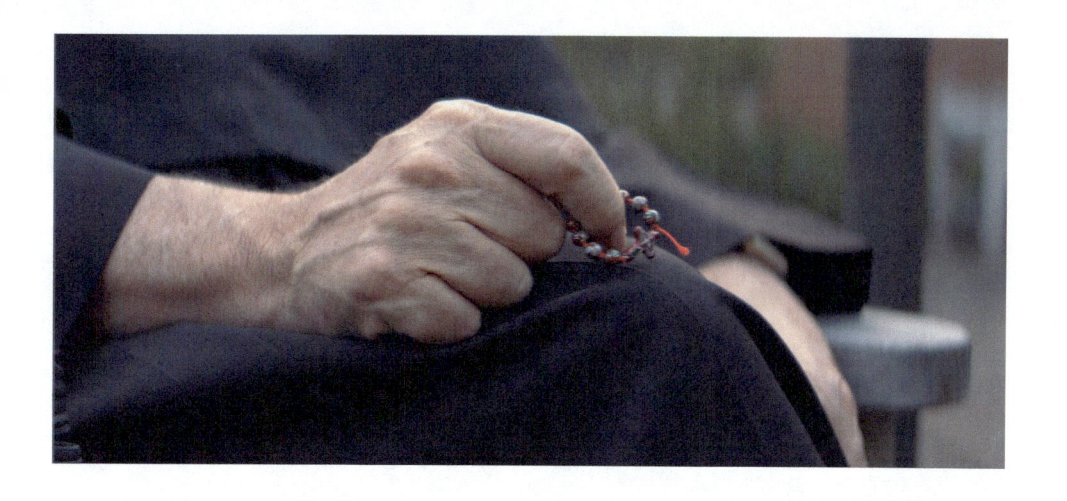

SENDING FORTH

Each of us has a vocation or a calling in life through which we sanctify others and ourselves at the service of God's Kingdom. Whether you are living it out currently or are discerning it in faithful discipleship, consider those areas in which fear (fear of what others may think, fear of being vulnerable and seen, fear of failure) is holding you back. How can a faithful, humble, trusting, simple, and more charitable disposition dispel the fear and open new means for God to work through you?

The Father Waits

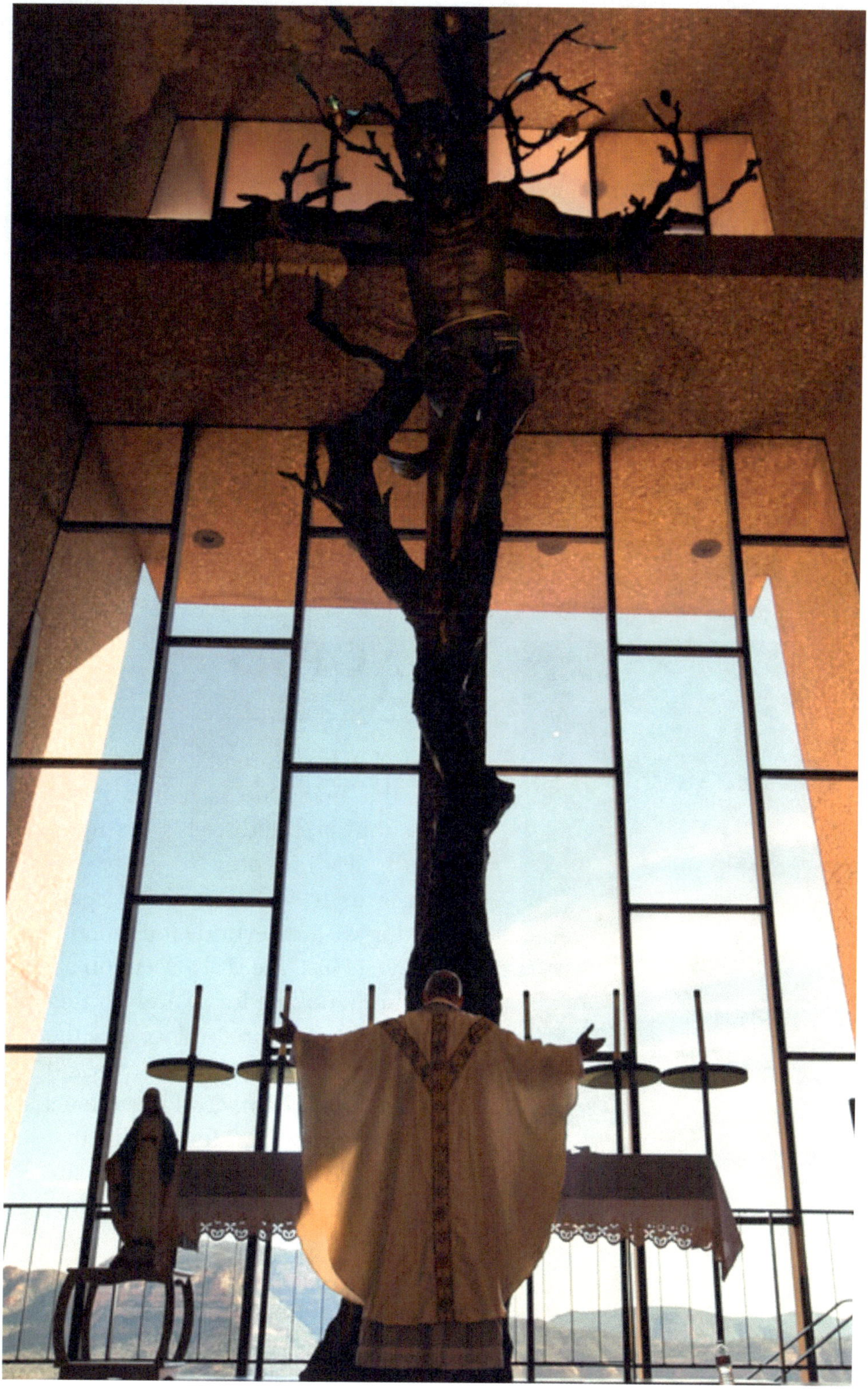

THE FATHER WAITS
EPISODE 6

SYNOPSIS

From the beginning, as Our Lord says, the Evil One is a liar. He is also cunning, building his lies upon a truth. Falling prey to these lies often leads to isolation and despair, thinking we are beyond God's mercy. However, His Gaze is always upon us. He is both looking for us and waiting for us, not giving up until we, like the Prodigal Son, come to our senses and find respite in Him. God permits us to wander, however, for it is in that experience that the innate desire of our hearts to return home to the Father can be enlightened. We must also come to realize that we, like the Elder Son, cannot earn the Love of the Father.

"Do not doubt, do not hesitate, never despair of the mercy of God."

- St. Isidore of Seville -

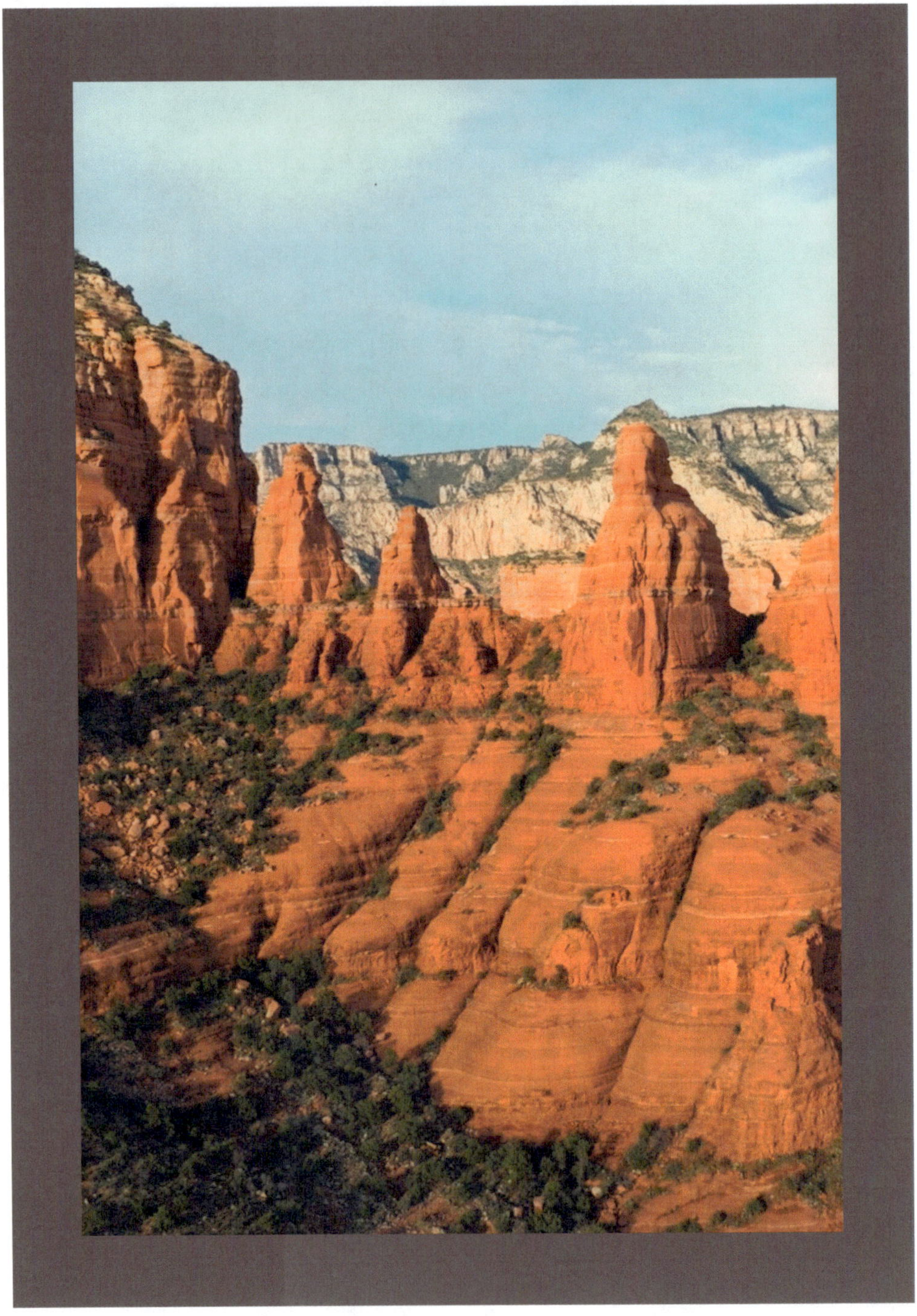

KEY TEXTS

"While he was still a long way off, his father caught sight of him, and was filled with compassion. He ran to his son, embraced him and kissed him." Luke 15:20

SAINTS

St. Margaret Mary Alacoque: "The Divine Heart is an ocean full of all good things, wherein poor souls can cast all their needs; it is an ocean full of joy to drown our sadness, an ocean of humility to drown our folly, an ocean of mercy to those in distress, an ocean of love in which to submerge our poverty."

St. Alphonsus Liguori: "What does it cost us to say, 'My God help me! Have mercy on me!' Is there anything easier than this?"

SCRIPTURE

John 8:42a, 44a: "Jesus said to them, 'If God were your Father, you would love me…You belong to your father the devil and you willingly carry out your father's desires. He was a murderer from the beginning and does not stand in truth, because there is no truth in him.'"

John 16:33: "In the world you will have trouble, but take courage, I have conquered the world."

Matthew 11:28: "Come to me, all you who labor and are burdened, and I will give you rest."

OTHER

Henri Nouwen: "I am the prodigal son every time I search for unconditional love where it cannot be found."

Peter Kreeft: "It is mercy, not justice or courage or even heroism, that alone can defeat evil."

Henri Nouwen: "Indeed, mercy is the central nucleus of the Gospel message; it is the very name of God, the Face with which he revealed himself in the Old Covenant and fully in Jesus Christ, the incarnation of creative and redemptive love."

"Enter through the narrow gate; for the gate is wide and the road broad that leads to destruction, and those who enter through it are many. How narrow the gate and constricted the road that leads to life. And those who find it are few."

Matthew 7:13-14

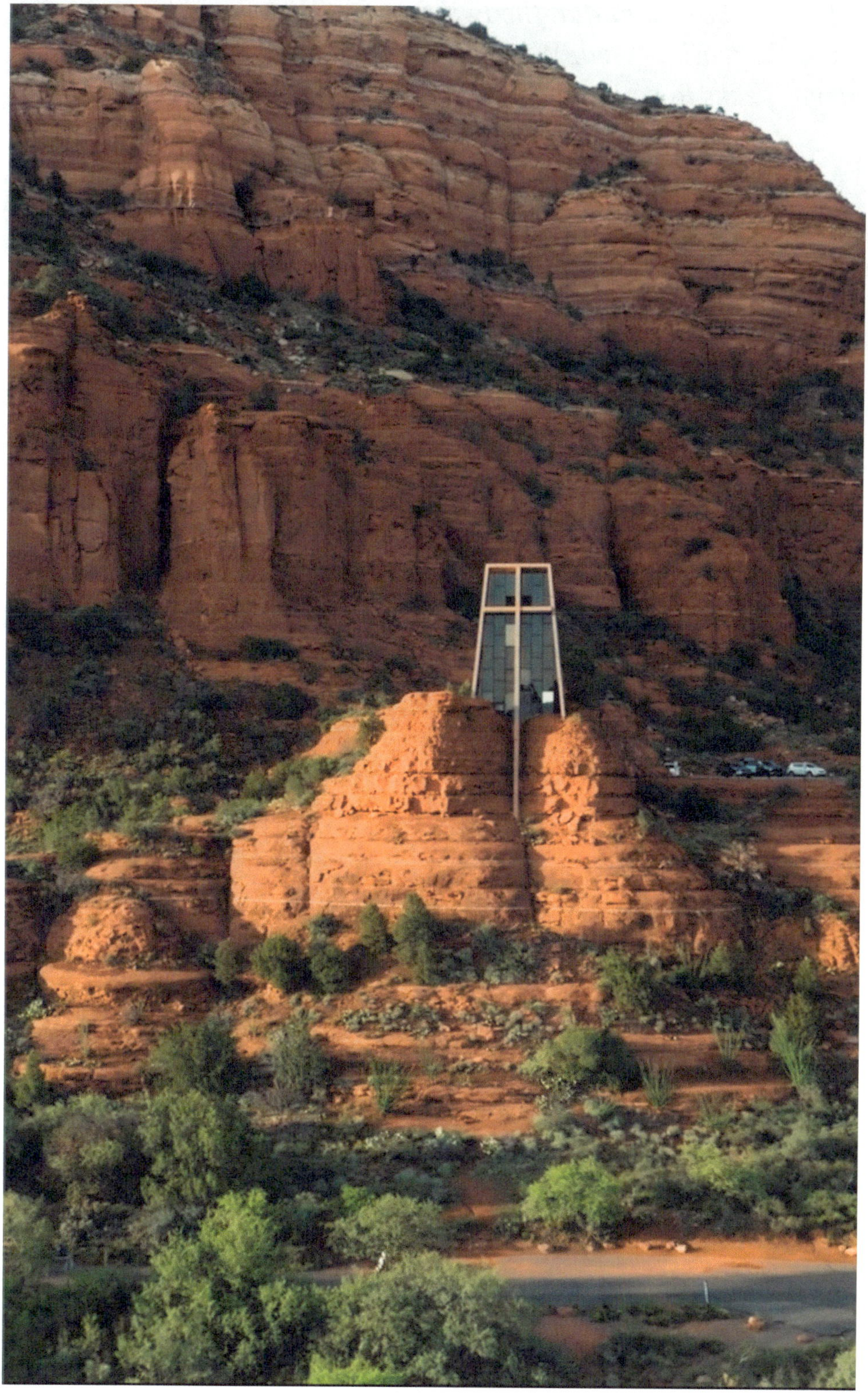

1. It has been said that the Evil One can not create; he can only twist the truth of God. What truths are at the center of the lies the devil speaks to you in temptation, and how can leaning into these truths help you to overcome them?

2. *Are there any sins in which you stubbornly think that you have to overcome them alone or, alternatively, that you can't possibly overcome them? Concretely speaking, what are some of the spiritual tools at hand that you are not taking advantage of?*

3. Henri Nouwen says, "I am the prodigal son every time I search for unconditional love where it cannot be found." Can you recall an experience of disappointment that came from searching for love in the wrong places? Where, now, are you doing the same, a road that will lead only to heartbreak, and what truth does the Father want to speak into the situation?

"God our Father, make us really alive by giving us the light to know You, the only true God, and Jesus Christ Whom You have sent. Grant us the Holy Spirit and enable us to speak volumes about Your ineffable mysteries."

Pause for Prayer

PRAYER BY SERAPION OF THMUIS

GOING

Dave VanVickle told the story of the power of the Sacrament of Reconciliation in his life to overcome a consistent, habitual sin. Are you committed to the power of God manifested through the encounter with the Risen Lord that is given by way of the sacraments? Or, alternatively, are they more like ritual boxes to check off?

DEEPER

Dr. Bob Schuchts tells a powerful story of the power of prayer and his father's conversion. Do you believe in the power of the Holy Spirit enough to trust that He can move and work in the hearts of those you love most? How often do you ignore God's promptings to pray, even though you know that others may need it?

Heather Khym speaks to the power of allowing God to whisper into our hearts the secrets of our identities. However, these kinds of whispers are not discernable above the noise of everyday life. Do you make time for silence and to read the Scriptures? If not, when and how will you possibly encounter the Lord who speaks most often in a still, small voice?

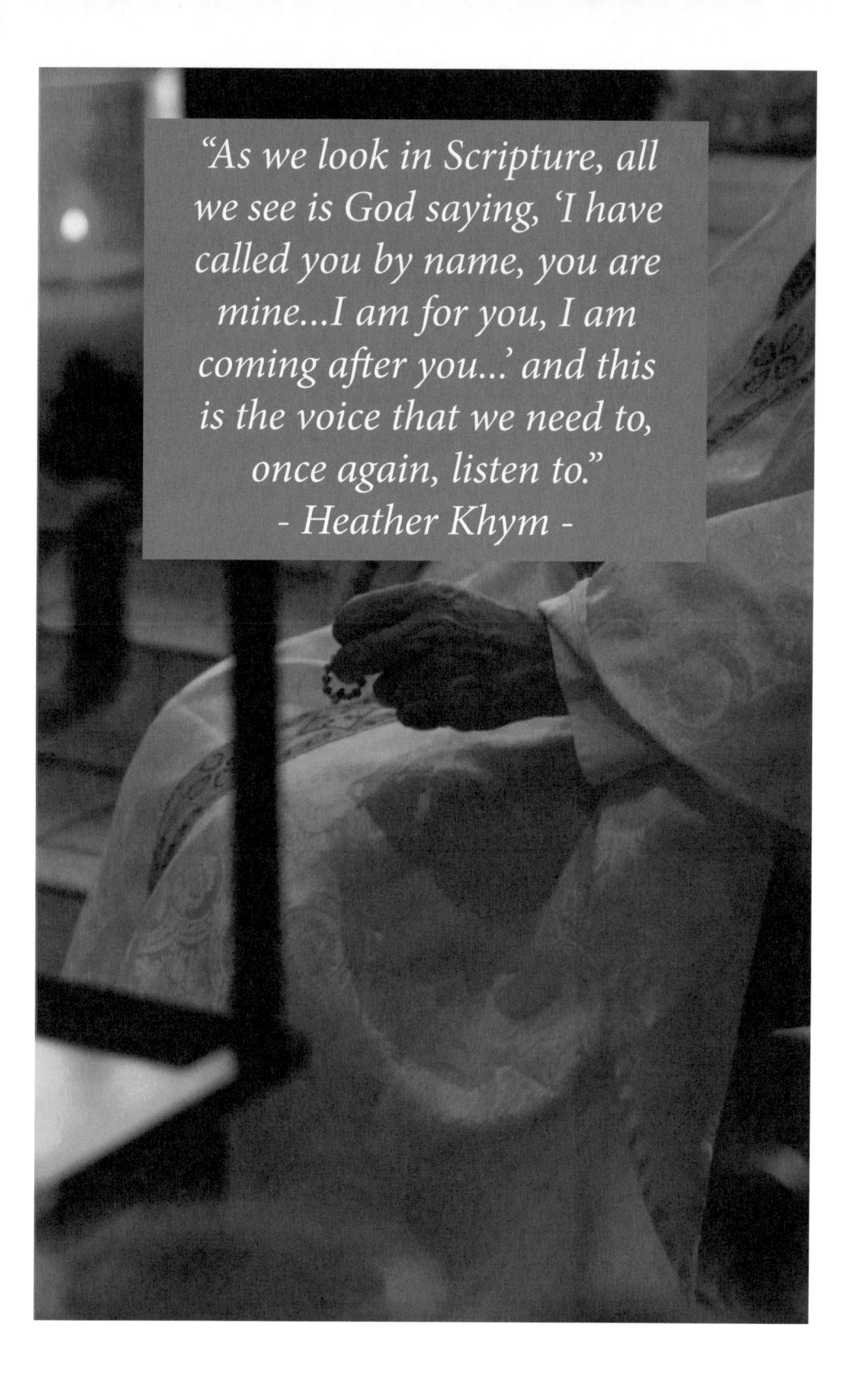

"As we look in Scripture, all we see is God saying, 'I have called you by name, you are mine...I am for you, I am coming after you...' and this is the voice that we need to, once again, listen to."
- Heather Khym -

REFLECTION BY HENRI NOUWEN

Excerpt from *The Return of the Prodigal Son*

The prodigal's return is full of ambiguities. He is traveling in the right direction, but what confusion! He admits that he was unable to make it on his own and confesses that he would get better treatment as a slave in his father's house than as an outcast in a foreign land, but he is still far from trusting his father's love. He knows that he is still the son, but tells himself that he has lost the dignity to be called "son," and he prepares himself to accept the status of a "hired man" so that he will at least survive...

One of the greatest challenges in the spiritual life is to receive God's forgiveness. There is something in us humans that keeps us clinging to our sins and prevents us from letting God erase our past and offer us a completely new beginning. Sometimes it even seems as though I want to prove to God that my darkness is too great to overcome. While God wants to restore me to the full dignity of sonship, I keep insisting that I will settle for being a hired servant...Receiving forgiveness requires a total willingness to let God be God and do all the healing, restoring, and renewing. As long as I want to do even a part of that myself, I end up

"Peace To All who
Chapel Hours
Gift Shop Hours
PLEASE MAINTAIN
IN THE CHAPEL
ROMAN CATHOLIC

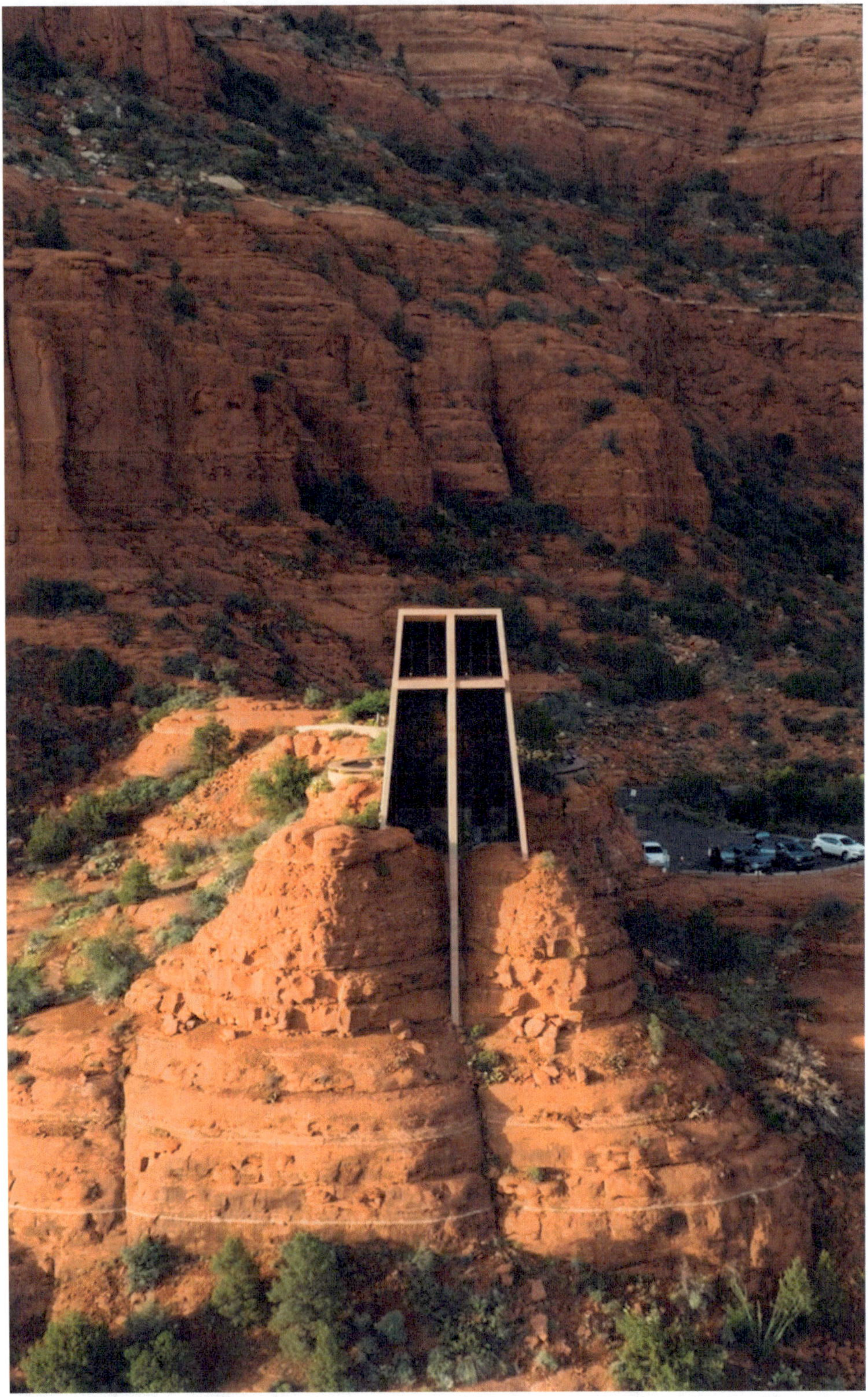

REFLECTION BY HENRI NOUWEN

with partial solutions, such as becoming a hired servant. As a hired servant, I can still keep my distance, still revolt, reject, strike, run away, or complain about my pay. As the beloved son, I have to claim my full dignity and begin preparing myself to become the father.

It is clear that the distance between the turning around and the arrival at home needs to be traveled wisely and with discipline. The discipline is that of becoming a child of God. Jesus makes it clear that the way to God is the same as the way to a new childhood. "Unless you turn and become like little children you will never enter the kingdom of Heaven." Jesus does not ask me to remain a child but to become one...

How can those who have come to this second childhood, this second innocence, be described? Jesus does this very clearly in the Beatitudes..."How blessed are the poor, the gentle, those who mourn, those who hunger and thirst for uprightness, the merciful, the pure of heart, the peacemakers, and those who are persecuted in the cause of uprightness."

These words present a portrait of the child of God. It is a self-portrait of Jesus, the Beloved Son. It is also a portrait of me as I must be.

REFLECT

Come, Holy Spirit. Often when we read and hear parables like the Parable of the Prodigal Son, we tend to identify ourselves too pridefully with the best of characters and their best moments. Similarly, we see the sins of those around us in the worst of characters and their immorality. Reflect on the words of Our Lord: "You hypocrite, remove the wooden beam from your eye first; then you will see clearly to remove the splinter from your brother's eye" (Matthew 7:5). Approach this parable by asking the Holy Spirit to enlighten your spiritual sense, not to build yourself up, but to grow in holiness as God desires.

SENDING FORTH

How often have each of us asked, "Where are you, God?" when He feels distant or unaware of our difficulties and circumstances? However, the first question God asks in the Bible is "Where are you?", which he poses to Adam and Eve after falling prey to the serpent's lies. If you have sinned and fallen prey to lies, take some time in quiet prayer to answer this question, for God desires reconciliation.

HEALING RESOURCES

My father's Father is a story of profound significance for all of us. Undoubtedly if you are here, you have been touched by the series and companion journal in a deep and significant way. It is our prayer for you that your relationship with God the Father would deepen through and as a result of this series, and that you can grow more and more into your identity as a son or a daughter of God the Father.

To that end, we recognize that you may be in need of additional resources, perhaps for healing or growth in your spirituality or your relationships. Here we have compiled some of the resources we know to be fruitful in these areas, mostly from those who contributed to *My father's Father*, but also from other sources that we know to be beneficial. However, if you feel that you are in need of guidance beyond the scope of these resources, then please reach out to a priest or a trusted therapist.

BOOKS

Be Healed: A Guide to Encountering the Powerful Love of Jesus in Your Life
by Dr. Bob Schuchts

Do You Want to Be Healed? A 10-Day Scriptural Retreat with Jesus
by Dr. Bob Schuchts

Finding Freedom in Christ: Healing Life's Hurts
by Dr. Matthew Breuninger

Abide: A Pathway to Transformative Healing and Intimacy With Jesus
by Heather Khym

Interior Freedom and *Trusting God in the Present* by Fr. Jaques Philippe

Loved as I Am: An Invitation to Conversion, Healing, and Freedom Through Jesus
by Sr. Miriam James Heidland, SOLT

Woman In Love: A Hope That Transforms
by Katie Hartfiel

PODCASTS

Restore the Glory
by Dr. Bob Schuchts and Jake Khym, MA
- In *Restore the Glory*, Dr. Schuchts and Jake Khym use their more than 50 years of combined experience to reach and accompany people into a fuller life of freedom by taking an integrated approach to the healing journey.

MORE RESOURCES

Known: Embraced by the Heart of the Father
by Dr. Matthew Brueninger and Isaac Wicker, MS
- *Known* is a 12-week online Catholic coaching program to heal wounded relationships with God the Father and rediscover an identity as beloved sons and daughters.

John Paul II Healing Center
featuring Dr. Bob Schuchts and Jake Khym, MA
- The John Paul II Healing Center offers healing conferences, retreats, books, and talks.

Life Restoration
by Jake and Heather Khym
- *Life Restoration* is centred on evangelization, healing, and unlocking the heart through healing conferences, retreats, books, and talks.

CatholicTherapists.com and The Catholic Psychotherapy Association
- Two online ways of finding a Catholic therapist who can help those in need of further healing.